Tales from Perrault

Tales from Perrault

Translated by Ann Lawrence

Illustrated by Tony James Chance

Oxford University Press

Oxford New York Toronto Melbourne

Charles Perrault's stories were first
translated into English as *Tales of Mother Goose*

Oxford University Press, Walton Street, Oxford OX2 6DP

Oxford New York Toronto
Delhi Bombay Calcutta Madras Karachi
Petaling Jaya Singapore Hong Kong Tokyo
Nairobi Dar es Salaam Cape Town
Melbourne Auckland

and associated companies in
Berlin Ibadan

Oxford is a trade mark of Oxford University Press

Text © Ann Lawrence 1988
Illustrations © Tony James Chance 1988

First published by Oxford University Press 1988

British Library Cataloguing in Publication Data
Lawrence, Ann
    Perrault.——(Oxford illustrated classics).
    I. Title   II. Perrault, Charles
    823'.914[J]   PZ8

ISBN 0–19–274533–6

Set by Pentacor Ltd, High Wycombe, Bucks
Printed in Hong Kong

Contents

Colour Plates

Facing page 86

The chariot could hardly move through the dense crowd.

Facing page 102

There was not a woman in the country, who did not prepare to present her finger.

For Mademoiselle Joan and
Madame her Mother

Charles Perrault's
Tales of Mother Goose

Introduction

MADAME la Marquise was leaving Paris for her estates in the country. The evening before her departure everything that was to go with her was packed, while most of the rooms in her town house were already shrouded in dust sheets and closed up.

'Look at us! Perching on boxes and eating off kitchen ware!' she cried, when her friend Monsieur Perrault, the Academician, called to wish her a safe journey. 'It's like camping on the edge of one's own life, Monsieur. Thank heavens I can still offer you the rudiments of hospitality – though I will not answer for the *quality* of supper tonight, nor for the elegance of its presentation.'

Monsieur Perrault smiled. The salon did certainly look a little bare and chilly, as if the life of the house had been packed with Madame's luggage, but he had no doubt that her standards of hospitality would be maintained even now.

Madame's young daughter joined them, and they supped informally in Madame's own room.

'Picnicking among the ruins,' she said tragically. 'How am I going to survive those long weeks away from Paris? But there's no help for it. There is business to be attended to, and no one else to attend to it. You will have to write to me regularly with all the news, otherwise I shall feel as if I am living in a desert.'

'You shall have whole gazettes of news, Madame,' Monsieur Perrault promised.

'Will you write to me, too, Monsieur?' the little Mademoiselle asked. 'No one tells stories like you do, and I shan't have any all the time we're away.'

'Very well: news for Madame, stories for Mademoiselle.' Monsieur Perrault laid his hand on his heart. 'Let me be cast out of your favour forever, if I fail.'

Madame shook her head.

'Monsieur, I am afraid you'll find no time for any other work, if you keep this promise.'

'So be it,' said Monsieur Perrault solemnly. 'But it shall be kept.'

'Can I have a story now?' Mademoiselle begged.

Madame glanced at the clock on her mantelshelf.

'My darling, you should be in bed,' she said. 'We start so early tomorrow.'

'It could be a very short one, Madame,' said Monsieur Perrault.

'A very short one, then,' said Madame.

So Monsieur Perrault began:

'There was once . . .'

Little Red Cap

THERE was once a little village girl, the prettiest you could hope to see. Her mother was foolishly fond of her, while her grandmother was even more so. This good woman had made for her a little red velvet hood which suited her so well that everyone around called her Little Red Cap.

One day when her mother had been baking and had made some scones, she said:

'Go and see how your grandmother is getting along. Someone told me she was ill, so take her some scones and this little pot of butter.'

Little Red Cap set off at once for her grandmother's home, which was in another village.

As she was passing through a wood, she met

Grandpa Wolf, who would have liked very much to have eaten her, but he dared not because of the woodcutters, who lived in the forest. He therefore asked her where she was going, and the poor child, who did not know that it is dangerous to stop for a conversation with a wolf, said:

'I'm going to see my grandmother, to take her some scones and a little pot of butter my mother has sent her.'

'Does she live very far away?' asked the wolf.

'Oh yes!' said Little Red Cap. 'It's way beyond the mill you see down there – right down there, by the first house in the village.'

'Well,' said the wolf. 'I'd like to go and see her too. I'll go by this path, and you go by that one, and we'll see who gets there first.'

The wolf set off along the shortest path, running with all his might, while the little girl went by the longest, amusing herself by gathering nuts, running after butterflies, and making up bunches of the small flowers she came across.

It was not long before the wolf arrived at the grand-mother's house. He knocked at the door: tap! tap!

'Who's there?'

'It's your little girl, Little Red Cap,' said the wolf, disguising his voice. 'I've brought you some scones and a little pot of butter, sent to you by my mother.'

The good grandmother, who was in bed, because she felt a little poorly, called out:

'Pull out the peg and lift the latch.'

The wolf drew out the peg and the door opened. At once he leapt on the worthy lady and devoured her in less than no time, as he had not eaten for more than three days. Then he shut the door and lay down in the grandmother's bed to wait for Little Red Cap, who arrived some time later and knocked at the door: tap! tap!

'Who's there?'

When Little Red Cap heard the big gruff voice of the wolf, she was afraid at first, but supposing that her grandmother must be hoarse from a bad cold, she replied:

'It's your little girl, Little Red Cap. I've brought you some scones and a little pot of butter, sent to you by my mother.'

Trying to sweeten his voice a shade, the wolf called out:

'Pull out the peg and lift the latch.'

Little Red Cap drew out the peg and the door opened.

Seeing her enter, the wolf hid under the bedcovers and said:

'Put the scones and the little pot of butter on the bread bin, and come into bed with me.'

Little Red Cap undressed and climbed into the bed, where she was astonished to see what her grandmother looked like without her clothes.

'Grandma, what big arms you've got!' she said.

'That's so I can hug you better, my child,' said the wolf.

'Grandma, what big legs you've got!'

'That's so I can run better, my little girl.'

'Grandma, what big ears you've got!'

'That's so I can hear better, my darling.'

'And Grandma, what big eyes you've got!'

'That's so I can see better, my sweet morsel.'

'But Grandma, what big teeth you've got!'

'That's so I can eat you!'

And so saying, the wicked wolf threw himself on Little Red Cap and ate her up.

'Oh, what a horrid story!' cried Mademoiselle. 'What about the woodcutters? Why couldn't they come and rescue Little Red Cap and her poor Granny?'

Monsieur Perrault shook his head dubiously.

'I've never heard of anyone being rescued from the belly of a wolf,' he said.

Madame looked severe.

'Now see what you've done, Monsieur,' she said. 'We shall have nightmares at the very least, and I shouldn't be surprised if we are afraid to leave the house all the time we're in the country!'

'*I* shan't be afraid,' said Mademoiselle stoutly. 'I'm not worried about silly wolves.'

'But perhaps you should be,' said Monsieur Perrault seriously. 'You can see from this story that children had better not listen to everyone they meet, and pretty, nicely brought up little girls should be particularly careful whom they talk to. If they're not, it's no wonder they get eaten up.

'Only I think you have less to fear from any wolves that may prowl in your mama's forests, than from the kind that may be found here in Paris! For there are all sorts of wolves, aren't there? Some of them have very civil dispositions – no growling, no snarling, nothing of sound and fury at all – they are so open and familiar, so obliging and pleasant, that they are allowed to attend young ladies right into their houses, even into their bedrooms. But, oh dear, who knows if these amiable wolves may not be the most dangerous of all!'

'I'd say there was no doubt about it,' said Madame, her lips tightening a little. 'Perhaps after all I should thank you for reminding us of the annoyances we are leaving behind along with the pleasures, when we set off for our desert.'

'Madame,' said Monsieur Perrault, rising. 'It is Paris which will be a desert without you.'

Dear Madame,

*   Although your letter in my hand was proof of your safe arrival its contents could not fail to fill me with horror, nonetheless. Your account of flooded roads, drunken coachmen and broken bridges made me positively shudder with apprehension for you. Thank God you are now safe at home.*

*   But my little Mademoiselle is already missing Paris, you say? She misses the company of young friends? I wonder what I can offer to lighten this long exile. Perhaps her fate might seem less heavy, if she compares it with that of another young lady, of whom I have heard tell. She was secluded in the country far longer than Mademoiselle, and in far more restricted circumstances . . .*

7

The Princess of
the Sleeping Wood

THERE was once a King and Queen who had no
children and they were more distressed by this than
I can tell you. They went to all the spas in the world
to drink the medicinal waters, they made vows and
went on pilgrimages, they were scrupulously devout
– in fact they tried everything, and nothing worked.
Eventually, however, the Queen did grow stout,
and gave birth to a daughter. A fine christening was
arranged, and all the Fays, who could be found in
the country (there were seven), were invited to be
godmothers to the little Princess, so that if each of
them gave her a gift, as was the custom of Fays at
that time, she would by this means be endowed
with every perfection imaginable.

(There is no need, I think, in these happy times, for me to tell you what Fays are, since I am sure your nurse will have told you about them from your earliest years.)

After the religious ceremonies the whole company returned to the King's palace, where he held a great banquet for the Fays. Their places at the table were magnificently laid, with a case of solid gold for each of them, containing a knife, fork and spoon of gold set with diamonds and rubies. But as they all took their seats, yet another Fay swept in – one whom no one had thought to invite, because she was extremely old, and, since it was more than fifty years since she had left the tower in which she lived, people had come to believe that she must be either dead or imprisoned there by magic.

Naturally the King had a place set for her immediately, but he had no means of giving her a case of solid gold like the others, as he had only ordered seven to be made, for the seven Fays who had been invited. It was all most embarrassing. There was nothing the King could do to convince the old lady that she had not been grossly insulted, and she sat down muttering under her breath.

One of the younger Fays happened to be sitting next to her, and gathered the impression, from the threatening tone of the old lady's resentful growls, that she was quite capable of wishing something troublesome on the little Princess. Therefore, when everyone left the table, she hid herself behind the tapestry, so that she could be sure of being the last to speak, and of having a chance to repair as far as possible any evil the old one might do.

Meanwhile the Fays began to bestow their gifts on the Princess. The gift of the youngest was that she should be the most beautiful creature in the world. The next said she should have the mind of an angel. The third promised that she should be graceful in everything she did, the fourth made her an exquisite dancer, the fifth granted that she should sing like a nightingale, and the sixth that she should play all sorts of musical instruments to perfection. Then came the turn of the eldest. Her head shaking as much from spite as from age, she declared that the Princess should one day run a spindle into her hand. And die of it.

The whole company shuddered with horror at this terrible gift, and there was no one present who did not weep. At that moment, however, the young Fay emerged from behind the tapestry.

'Be reassured, Your Majesties,' she said in a clear voice. 'Your daughter shall not die. It is true that I am not powerful enough to undo completely what my elder colleague has done: the Princess certainly will pierce her hand with a spindle, there is no avoiding that. But instead of dying, she will only fall into a deep sleep, which will last for a hundred years, at the end of which a king's son will come to wake her.'

In spite of the young Fay's words, the King was determined to avert the misfortune foretold by the old lady. He immediately published an edict forbidding anyone to spin with a spindle, or even to have one in the house, on pain of death.

Fifteen or sixteen years passed by. The King and Queen were taking a holiday in one of their country houses, and it happened one day that, having nothing else to do, the Princess began to explore the old castle. She ran from room to room, always climbing upwards, until she reached the top of the keep, where in a little attic she found an old woman, all alone, spinning from her distaff. She had been the King's mother's nurse, and having lived tucked away in her attic for as long as anyone could remember, she had been even more completely forgotten than the ancient Fay. Being also as deaf as a post, she had never heard a word of the King's orders against spinning with a spindle.

'What are you doing there, goodwife?' the Princess shouted in her ear.

'I'm spinning, my lovely,' replied the old woman, who did not recognise her.

'How pretty it is!' said the Princess. 'How do you do it? Give it to me and let me see if I can do it so nicely.'

She took the spindle and began to twirl it vigorously, but of course, having never so much as seen one in her life before, she had no idea how to handle it. She had hardly started, when, being over hasty and a little clumsy (and anyway it was ordained by the Decree of the Fays), she drove the spindle into her hand, and fell fainting.

The good old woman was greatly distressed and shouted for help. People came running from all sides. They threw water in the Princess's face, they unlaced her, they slapped her hands, they rubbed her temples with Queen of Hungary's Water, but nothing would revive her.

Then the King, who had climbed up to the keep to see what all the noise was about, remembered the Fays' predictions. Realising that all must have happened as they had said, he had the Princess placed in the most handsome apartment in the palace, on a bed hung with gold and silver embroideries.

She was so beautiful, you might have said she was an angel, for her faint had not drained the lively colour from her complexion: her cheeks were still rosy, her lips like coral. Her eyes were closed, but the sound of her gentle breathing proved that she was not dead.

The King commanded that she be allowed to sleep in peace, until the hour of her awakening should come.

At the time this accident befell the Princess, the good Fay, who had saved her life by condemning her to sleep for a hundred years, was in the Kingdom of Mataquin, twelve thousand leagues away. However, she was advised in an instant of what had happened by a little dwarf in her service, who had a pair of seven league boots (these were boots in which one could cover seven leagues with a single stride). She departed immediately, and appeared an hour later in a chariot of fire drawn by dragons. The King went to meet her and handed her down from her carriage.

She inspected all the arrangements he had made, and approved of them as far as they went, but being a lady of great foresight and good sense, she realised that the Princess would be terribly confused and helpless, if she were to wake all alone in this old castle. So this is what she did.

She touched everyone in the castle (except the King and the Queen) with her ring – housekeepers, maids of honour, ladies-in-waiting, gentlemen, officers, stewards, chefs, undercooks, scullions, guards, gatekeepers, pages, footmen – every single one. She also touched all the horses in the stables, along with their grooms. She touched the great guard dogs in the outer courtyard and little Pouffe, the Princess's pet dog, who lay beside her on her bed. From the moment she touched them, they all fell asleep, only to awake in the same moment as their mistress, so as to be all ready to serve her when she should have need of them. Even the spits by the kitchen fire, all loaded with partridges and pheasants, stopped turning, and the fire itself fell asleep too. All this was done in a moment. The Fairy kind do not take long over their work.

Then the King and Queen, having kissed their dear child without her waking, left the castle, and published orders forbidding anyone to approach it. These prohibitions were not necessary, however, for within a quarter of an hour there grew up all around the park such a great number of trees large and small, and such a mass of brambles and thorn bushes interlaced one with another, that neither man nor beast could have passed through. Nothing of the castle could be seen but the very tops of the towers, and only from a good distance at that. No one had the least doubt that the Fay had performed yet another trick of her trade, so that the Princess might have nothing to fear from the curious, while she slept.

Many things change in a hundred years. At the end of that time the King who then reigned in the country, was of another family than that of the sleeping Princess, and the world of the Court had completely forgotten her. So it was that when the King's son went hunting in that area, he was intrigued by the towers he saw rising above a vast, thick wood, and asked what they were. No one really knew, but each replied according to the tales they had heard. Some said it was an old castle haunted by ghosts, others that all the witches and warlocks of the country met there for their Sabbath. The most common opinion was that it was inhabited by an ogre, who carried there all the children he could capture, in order to be able to eat them at his leisure, without anyone being able to follow him, since he alone had the power to make a way through the forest.

The Prince was at a loss to know what to make of this, when an old peasant spoke up.

'Your Highness, I heard my father say more than fifty years ago, that the most beautiful princess imaginable was in that castle, bound by enchantment to sleep for a hundred years, until she could be wakened by the King's son, for whom she was intended.'

These words set the young prince all aflame. He needed no time to weigh the matter: he knew at once that he must be the one to bring such a fine adventure to its conclusion, and urged on by love and ambition for glory, he resolved on the spot to see whatever there was to be seen.

He had hardly taken more than a step towards the wood, when all the great trees, the brambles and the thorn bushes parted of their own accord to let him pass. He was in a wide avenue, at the end of which stood a castle. He began to walk towards it, but when he looked round, he was surprised to see that none of his people had been able to follow him, because the trees had closed together again as soon as he had gone by. He did not hesitate to continue on his way, however: a prince, young and in love (even if he does not know with whom) is always valiant.

He entered a great forecourt, where everything that first met his eyes was enough to freeze him with fear. The silence was terrifying. The very image of Death presented itself on all sides, for there was nothing to be seen anywhere but the bodies of men and animals, sprawled lifeless on the ground. Nevertheless, when he looked at the blotchy noses and florid faces of the gatekeepers, it became clear to him that they were only asleep, and the cups they held, in which there were still a few drops of wine, showed that they had fallen asleep while drinking.

From there he passed into a great courtyard paved with marble. He climbed a staircase to the guardroom, where the guards were drawn up in ranks, carbines shouldered and snoring their heads off. He crossed several rooms full of ladies and gentlemen, all asleep, though some were standing while others were seated. And then, in the very heart of the castle, he came to a room, gilded all over, where he saw the most beautiful sight he had ever seen. There on the bed, the curtains of which were open on all sides, lay a princess some fifteen or sixteen years old, as it seemed, whose dazzling fairness had something luminous, even divine about it. He approached, trembling and full of wonder, and fell on his knees beside her.

Then, since the end of the enchantment had come, the Princess awoke, and looking at him with eyes more tender than seemed possible for a first glance, she said:

'Is it you, my Prince? I have waited for you a long time.'

The Prince was so charmed by these words, and even more by the manner in which they were spoken, that he did not know how to express his joy and gratitude. He assured her that he loved her more than himself, and though I fear his speech was poorly composed, I think it must have been all the more pleasing on that account: the more love, the less eloquence, they say. He was more confused, indeed, than she, which is hardly surprising, for she had had time enough to think about what she would say to him when this moment came. It seems, you see (though History says nothing of it), that the good Fay had arranged for her to enjoy pleasant dreams during her long sleep.

In the end they talked for four hours, and still had not told each other half the things they had to tell.

Meanwhile the whole palace had woken with the Princess, each person only thinking of taking up his duties where they had been broken off, but since they were not all in love, they were near dying of hunger. The Lady of the Bedchamber, as anxious as the others for her first meal in a hundred years, finally lost patience, and told the Princess in a loud voice, that dinner was served.

The Prince helped the Princess to her feet. She was fully dressed, and very magnificently too, but the Prince observed that she was dressed in the fashion of his great grandmother's youth. He was careful not to tell her this, however, nor to comment on her old-fashioned manners, which seemed very formal and quaint to him. She was no less beautiful for that.

They proceeded to a dining room with mirrors all round the walls, where they supped, waited on by the Princess's servants. Violins and oboes played old tunes, which still had not lost their charm, though no one else had played them in nearly a hundred years. After supper, without wasting any time, the chaplain married them in the castle chapel, and the Lady of the Bedchamber drew the curtains on them.

They slept little: the Princess did not have much need of sleep, after all, and the Prince left her at dawn to return to the city, where his father must be anxious about him by this time.

On his return the Prince told his father that he had lost his way in the forest, and that he had slept in the hut of a charcoal burner, who had fed him on black bread and cheese. As for the mysterious towers — he shrugged, nothing but an old ruin; the only mystery there was why anyone should ever have thought the place interesting in any way.

Being a straightforward, good-natured man, the King believed him, but his mother was not so easily persuaded. Seeing that he now went hunting every day, and that he could always find a ready excuse for staying out all night —

even two or three nights together at times – she did not doubt that he had a lady friend.

The Prince lived with the Princess in this fashion for more than two whole years, and had two children by her, of which the first, a daughter, was named Dawn, and the second, a son, was named Day, because he seemed even more beautiful than his sister.

The Queen tried several times to coax her son into explaining himself, but he never dared to confide his secret to her. He feared her, even though he loved her, for she was of the ogress kind, and it was said that the King had only married her because of her great wealth. It was even whispered in the Court, that she still had ogre-like inclinations, and that when she saw small children pass by, she had the greatest difficulty in the world restraining herself from falling on them. Consequently the Prince was reluctant ever to say anything about his little family.

However, at the end of these two years the King died. When the Prince realised that he was at last his own master, he announced his marriage to the world, and went with great pomp to fetch the Queen, his wife, from her castle. She was given a magnificently ceremonious welcome to the Capital City, which she entered with her children on either side of her.

Some time after this, the King went to war against his neighbour, the Emperor of Cantalabutte. He left the regency of the realm to his Mother, and earnestly commended his wife and children to her care.

He was expected to be at the war all summer, and the moment he left, the Queen Mother sent her daughter-in-law and her children to a remote country house, surrounded by woods, the more easily to appease her horrible longing. She went there herself some days later, and one evening she said to her steward:

'Tomorrow for my dinner I want to eat little Dawn.'

'But Madame – !' said the steward.

16

'That is what I want,' said the Queen (and she said it in the tone of an ogress, who pines for young flesh). 'And I want to eat her with mustard and onion sauce.'

The poor man saw only too well that it was not advisable to offend an ogress, and so he took his big knife and climbed up to little Dawn's bedroom. She was then four years old, and came skipping and laughing to throw her arms round his neck, and beg a sweet from him. He burst into tears, the knife fell from his hand, and he went down into the farmyard, to cut the throat of a little lamb, for which he made such a good sauce, that his mistress assured him she had never eaten anything so good. Meanwhile he had carried off little Dawn, and had given her to his wife to hide in her lodging behind the farmyard.

A week later the wicked Queen said to her steward:

'For my supper tonight I want to eat little Day.'

He said nothing this time, but resolved to deceive her as before. He went to look for little Day, and found him with a small foil in his hand, fencing with a fat monkey. He was no more than three years old. The steward took him to his wife, who hid him with Dawn, and in place of Day he served up a very tender little kid, which the ogress found wonderfully tasty.

Things had gone very well up to then, but one evening this wicked Queen said to the steward:

'I want to eat the Queen now, in the same sauce as her children.'

At this the poor steward despaired of being able to deceive her again. The young Queen was more than twenty (not counting the hundred years she had slept); her skin, though white and beautiful, was surely a little tough, and was it possible to find a beast as tough as that? He decided that if he were to save his own life, he would have to cut the Queen's throat, and he climbed the stairs to her room with the intention of doing the terrible job properly this time. He worked himself into a passion, and entered the young

Queen's chamber, poignard in hand. However, he did not want to startle her, and so he told her with great respect the order he had received from the Queen Mother.

'Do it, do it!' she said, offering him her neck. 'Execute the order you have been given. I shall go to see my children again, my poor little children, that I loved so much.' (She believed them to be dead, since someone had taken them away without telling her anything.)

'No, no, Madame,' replied the poor steward, altogether softened. 'You shall not die. You shall indeed see your dear children again, however, but it will be in my home, where I have hidden them, and I will trick the Queen once more, by making her eat a young doe in your place.'

He led her at once to his lodging, where he left her to embrace and weep over her children, then he went to dress a doe for the table. The Queen ate it for her supper with as good an appetite as if it really had been her daughter-in-law. She was well satisfied with her cruelty, and was preparing to tell the King on his return that rabid wolves had eaten his wife and children.

One evening, however, while she was prowling the courtyards and farmyards of the castle, as was her habit, hoping to sniff out fresh meat, she heard little Day crying in a basement room, because the Queen his mother meant to whip him, for being naughty. She also heard little Dawn asking pardon for her brother. When she recognised the voices of the Queen and her children, the ogress was furious at having been deceived.

First thing the following morning, in a dreadful voice which made the whole world tremble, she ordered that a great vat be taken to the middle of the courtyard, and filled with toads, vipers, lizards and serpents, intending that the Queen and her children, the steward, his wife and his servant should be thrown into it. She commanded them to be brought out with their hands tied behind their backs.

They were already standing there, and the executioners

were preparing to throw them into the vat, when the King, who had not been expected so soon, rode into the courtyard having travelled post haste. He was utterly astounded by the horrible spectacle which met his eyes, and demanded to be told the meaning of it. At first no one replied, because no one dared to explain the situation to him, but then the ogress, maddened to see her plan foiled, threw herself head first into the vat, and was devoured in an instant by the venomous beasts, with which it had been filled at her orders.

The King could hardly fail to be upset by this – she was his mother, when all was said and done – but he very soon found consolation with his beautiful wife and children.

. . . Now, I think one might say it is reasonable enough to expect to have to wait a little while for a husband, who is rich, handsome, gallant, tender and so on – but to wait a hundred years, and asleep all that time? I think that really would be something to complain about, dear Mademoiselle. In fact, I'm pretty sure the woman is not to be found, who would be able to sleep so peacefully. What do you think?

Anyway, it seems to me that this tale should make us appreciate that the joys of marriage are no less happy for being deferred, and that one loses nothing by waiting. But when young ladies aspire to the state of conjugal felicity with such enthusiasm, I really cannot have the heart to preach such a moral to them, can I?

As to my news, Madame, all the news is that your friends have been waiting for news of you. And now *your* adventures will be all that is talked about here, until everyone has had the opportunity to tremble for you . . .

Dear Madame,

So Mademoiselle was not impressed by my story of the Sleeping Princess? She thinks that because one poor girl had to wait a hundred years for a husband, that is no reason why she herself should be left on the shelf? And when you pointed out to her that a lady so very young was hardly in danger of that, what was her response? No doubt she cited innumerable instances of ladies betrothed, if not married, before they were her age. But were they any happier in the long run? And how many, who are so anxious to marry, have time enough later to regret their haste?

Perhaps a cautionary tale on the subject might be in order.

There is also something to be said about another little failing, which may have something to do with my little friend's impatience: curiosity. It always costs more grief than it is worth. You see a thousand examples of it every day. And it is such a trivial pleasure, too: the moment it is gratified, the object of it ceases to be of any interest.

However, to the story . . .

Bluebeard

THERE was once a man who owned beautiful houses both in Town and in the country, equipped with tableware of gold and silver, embroidered furnishings and carriages gilded all over. Unfortunately, however, he also had a blue beard, which bizarre adornment gave him such a hideous and terrifying appearance, that there was no woman, young or old, who did not shun him.

He had a neighbour in Town, a lady of good family (but no great wealth), who had two perfectly lovely daughters, and when they were both of an age to marry, he asked her if he might take one of them for his wife, leaving to her the choice of which she thought best to give him. The two girls were not at all enthusiastic about the idea, and they passed the matter to and fro from one to the other, neither being able to bring herself to accept a man with a blue beard. They were further repelled by the fact that he was known to have been married several times before, but no one knew what had become of his former wives.

In order to make their acquaintance, Bluebeard took them with their mother and three or four of their best friends, along with several other young people of the neighbourhood, to one of his country houses, where they stayed for a week. The whole visit was nothing but a succession of hunting and fishing parties, excursions, dances, banquets, picnics. No one slept at all, and the nights were spent in playing practical jokes on each other. In short, everything went off so well, that the younger girl began to find that the master of the house did not have such a very blue beard after all, and that he was very courteous and cultivated. As soon as they returned to the town, the marriage was concluded.

At the end of a month Bluebeard told his wife that he was obliged to take a trip of at least six weeks into the provinces, on a business matter of some importance. He begged her to enjoy herself thoroughly in his absence; she must have her friends to stay, she should take them to the country if she felt so inclined, but above all she must keep cheerful, whatever she did.

'Take my keys,' he said. 'Here are the keys of the two big store-rooms, these are for the chests of gold and silver plate which aren't in everyday use, these are for my strong-boxes in which my gold and silver coin is kept, these are for my jewel caskets, and here is the master key to all the rooms. As for this little key here, it is the key to the small room at the end of the long gallery on the ground floor. Open everything, go everywhere you please – except into that one small room. I forbid you to enter it. I forbid it in the strongest possible terms, and I warn you now, that if you do come to open it, there is no saying what I may do in my anger.'

She promised to observe all his orders to the letter, and having kissed her goodbye, he climbed into his carriage and set off on his journey.

The young bride's neighbours and friends did not wait for an invitation to visit her, such was their impatience to see all the riches of her house (they had not dared to go there while her husband was at home, being intimidated by his blue beard). All at once there they were, wandering through the bedrooms, the ante-rooms, the dressing-rooms, each one richer and more beautiful than the one before. They climbed then to the store-rooms, where they could not sufficiently admire the number and beauty of the tapestries, the bed furnishings, the couches, the cabinets, the tables large and small, and the full-length mirrors, the frames of which (some of glass, others of silver and silver gilt) were the most elegant and magnificent ever seen. All the time they never stopped telling their friend how extravagantly lucky she was and how they envied her. But she, meanwhile, was not the least bit interested in all these riches, because of her impatience to go and open the small room on the ground floor.

So driven was she by her curiosity, that without considering how impolite it was to leave her visitors, she went down by a little secret staircase, taking it in such headlong haste that she risked breaking her neck two or three times. Having arrived at the door, however, she paused a while, thinking about her husband's prohibition, and considering what misfortune could possibly befall her, should she disobey; but the temptation was so great, that she could not overcome it. She took the little key therefore, and, trembling, opened the door.

At first she saw nothing, because the windows were shuttered, but after a few moments her eyes became accustomed to the poor light, and she saw that the floor was covered all over with congealed blood, dark and shining, so that it reflected the images of the dead women, whose bodies were fastened along the walls. (These were all the women

Bluebeard had married, and whose throats he had cut one after another.) She thought she would die of fright, and the key, which she had just withdrawn from the lock, fell from her hand, as she stood there aghast.

When she had recovered her wits a little, she picked up the key, closed the door again, and went up to her room to compose herself, but she was so upset that she found it impossible.

As she was trying to pull herself together she noticed that the key of the little room was stained with blood. Realising how this must betray her, she attempted two or three times to wipe it clean, but the blood would not go away. In vain she washed it, even rubbed it with fine sand and pumice stone, but whatever she did the blood still remained, for the key was enchanted, and there was no way of cleaning it completely. When the blood was removed from one side, it reappeared on the other.

That very evening Bluebeard returned from his journey. He said that he had received letters on the road, informing him that the business for which he had left home, had just been settled in his favour. His wife did everything she could to demonstrate her delight at his quick return.

The next day he asked her for his keys, and she gave them to him, but with such a trembling hand, that he guessed without any trouble all that had happened.

'Why is it,' he said, 'that the key to the little room is not with the others?'

'I must have left it upstairs on my table,' she said.

'Be sure to give it to me immediately,' said Bluebeard.

And although she made several attempts to divert him, she was eventually obliged to fetch the key.

Having examined it, Bluebeard said to his wife:

'Why is there blood on this key?'

'I don't know anything about it,' replied the poor girl, paler than death.

'You don't know anything about it!' Bluebeard repeated.

'But I know very well. You have dared to enter my room!
Well Madame, you shall enter it again, and take your place
alongside the other ladies you saw there.'

She threw herself at her husband's feet, weeping and
begging his pardon with every indication that she repented of
her disobedience. Beautiful and distressed as she was, she
would have softened a rock; but Bluebeard had a heart
harder than any rock.

'You must die, Madame,' he said. 'And at once.'

'Since I must die,' she replied, gazing at him with eyes full
of tears, 'give me at least a little time to pray.'

'You may have a quarter of an hour,' said Bluebeard.
'But not a moment more.'

When she was alone, she called to her sister and said:

'Sister Anne, I beg you, go up to the top of the tower to see
if there is any sign of our brothers. They promised that they
would come and see me today, so if you see them, signal to
them to hurry.'

Her sister climbed to the top of the tower, and from time
to time the poor distressed girl called to her:

'Anne, Sister Anne, do you see no one coming?'

And her sister Anne replied:

'I see nothing but the Sun which turns the earth to dust,
and the grass which covers it with green.'

Meanwhile Bluebeard, taking a great cutlass in his hand,
was shouting to his wife at the top of his voice:

'Come down quickly, or I shall come up!'

'A moment more, please,' replied his wife, and at once she
called softly: 'Anne, Sister Anne, do you see nothing yet?'

And her sister Anne replied:

'I see nothing but the Sun which turns the earth to dust
and the grass which covers it with green.'

'Now come down quickly,' shouted Bluebeard. 'Or I shall
come up.'

'I am coming,' said his wife, and then she called: 'Anne,
Sister Anne, do you still see nothing?'

'I see a great cloud of dust coming this way,' said her sister.

'Is it my brothers?'

'Alas no, sister, it is a flock of sheep.'

'Will you never come down?' roared Bluebeard.

'Only a moment more,' his wife replied, and then she cried: 'Anne, Sister Anne, do you see nothing at all?'

'I see two riders coming this way,' said her sister. 'But they are still a very long way off . . . God be praised!' she exclaimed a moment later. 'They are our brothers! I'll signal to them as best I can to hurry up!'

Bluebeard shouted then so loudly that the whole house shook. His poor wife went down and threw herself at his feet all weeping and dishevelled.

'This will do no good,' said Bluebeard. 'You must die.'

Then seizing her by the hair with one hand, he raised the cutlass in the air with the other, and was about to strike off her head. The poor girl turned towards him, and looking at him with fainting eyes, begged him to give her a brief moment to re-collect herself.

'No, no,' he said. 'Commend yourself to God.'

And raising his arm . . .

But at that moment someone knocked so loudly at the door, that Bluebeard stopped short. The door was flung open, and suddenly two cavaliers appeared. They drew their swords and ran straight at Bluebeard.

He recognised them as his wife's brothers, one a dragoon, the other a musketeer, and knowing that he had been unmasked, he at once fled for his life. The two brothers pursued him so closely, however, that they caught him before he could reach the stairs. They passed their swords right through his body and left him dead.

The poor young wife, meanwhile, was almost as near death as her husband, and did not have the strength to rise and embrace her brothers.

It was found in due course, that Bluebeard had no heirs,

and so his wife remained mistress of his entire fortune. Some of this she used to provide her sister with a dowry, so that she could marry a young nobleman, who had loved her for a long time. She also bought commissions in the army for her two brothers, and the rest of her wealth provided for her own marriage to an excellent gentleman, who made her forget the fearful time she had experienced with Bluebeard.

Dear Madame,

Mademoiselle's complaint, that I was trying to put her off marriage altogether, is surely most unjust. She will not yet have had the opportunity to study manners here in Paris, and you, in your country retreat, may have forgotten already what they are like, but I observe them daily, and so I am able to assure her, that no such thing could possibly happen to a young lady now.

Not that one need be very deeply read in the arcane mysteries of Society, to realise that this is a tale of Long Ago. I really do not believe such a terrible bridegroom could exist these days, nor one who would demand the impossible, or be ill-natured and jealous. These days a husband is usually the most docile of creatures in his wife's company, and whatever colour his beard, it would be hard to tell which of the two is master.

I am beginning to fear that my tales are less pleasing than I had hoped, nevertheless I will try once more. This time I think the moral is unimpeachable, for it shows that however great an advantage it may be to come into a fortune, talent, application and ingenuity are worth more to a young man than inherited wealth . . .

The Master Cat

THERE was once a miller, who had nothing by way
of fortune to leave to his three sons when he died,
except his mill, his donkey and his cat. The division
of the property was soon made, without any appeal
to lawyer or magistrate, who would have eaten up
the whole meagre inheritance in no time. The eldest
son had the mill, the second the donkey, and the
youngest had only the cat.

This third son could find no comfort in the
wretched lot which had fallen to him.

'My brothers will be able to earn a good enough
living by getting together,' he said. 'But as for me,
once I've eaten my cat and made myself a muff out
of his skin, I'm bound to die of hunger.'

The cat, who was listening to this speech but pretending not to, said with a serious, self-possessed air:

'There is no need at all for you to worry, Master. You only need to give me a bag, and have a pair of boots made for me, so that I can go through thick undergrowth in comfort, and you shall see that you did not get such a bad deal as you thought.'

Although the cat's master did not have much confidence in his claims, he had seen him perform so many slippery tricks in order to catch rats and mice – as when he hung by the feet, or hid in the flour to make his kill – that he did not altogether despair of finding relief from his wretched state of poverty.

When the cat had what he had asked for, he put on his boots. Slinging his bag round his neck, he took hold of the cords with his two front paws, and thus elegantly shod, he went off to a warren he knew, where there was a great number of rabbits. He put bran and wild lettuce in his bag, and stretching out on the ground as if he were dead, he waited until some young rabbit, little acquainted as yet with the deceits of this world, should come and poke its nose into his bag to eat what he had made so enticingly available.

He had hardly lain down, before his scheme met with success. A young fool of a rabbit entered his bag, and the Master Cat, drawing up the cords immediately, caught and killed it without mercy.

Glorying in his spoils, he went to the King's palace and asked for an audience. He was taken up to the State Apartments, where on entering he made a deep bow to the King and said:

'Sire, here is a rabbit from the warren of Monsieur le Marquis de Carabas – ' (this was the fanciful name he had picked at random to give to his master) ' – who charged me to present it to you on his behalf.'

'Tell your master that I thank him,' replied the King. 'And that it pleases me.'

On another occasion he went and hid in a wheat field, holding his bag open all the time, and when two partridges wandered into it, he pulled up the cords and caught both of them. He then went and presented them to the King, as he had the rabbit. The King received the two partridges with as much pleasure, and gave him a tip.

The cat continued in this way for two or three months, visiting the King from time to time to take him game from his master's hunting. Then one day, when he knew that the King was going for a drive along the river bank with his daughter, the most beautiful princess in the world, he said to his master:

'If you follow my advice, your fortune is made. You have only to bathe in the river, at the place I shall show you, and then leave the rest to me.'

The newly made Marquis de Carabas did what his cat advised, without having any idea what use it would be. While he was bathing, the King came past, and the cat started shouting at the top of his voice:

'Help! Help! Monsieur le Marquis de Carabas is drowning here!'

At this cry the King put his head out of the carriage window, and recognising the cat, who had brought him game so many times, he ordered his guards to hasten to the aid of Monsieur le Marquis de Carabas.

As they were dragging the poor Marquis out of the river, the Master Cat approached the carriage, and told the King that thieves had come while his master had been bathing, and had stolen his clothes, although he had shouted *stop thief!* with all his might. (The scamp had hidden them under a big stone.)

At once the King ordered the gentlemen of his wardrobe to go and find one of his finest suits for Monsieur le Marquis de Carabas. The King paid the young man a thousand compliments, and the beautiful clothes which were brought for him displayed his good looks so effectively (for he was handsome and well-built), that the King's daughter found him very much to her liking. Indeed, the Marquis de Carabas had not cast more than two or three glances in her direction, all very respectful and a little tenderly appealing, before she fell quite distractedly in love with him.

The King desired him to get into the carriage and join them in their excursion. The cat, delighted to see his plan beginning to succeed, went on ahead, and encountering some peasants cutting hay in a meadow, he said to them:

'Good mowers, if you do not tell the King that this meadow you are mowing belongs to Monsieur le Marquis de Carabas, you will all be chopped up as fine as meat for a pâté.'

When the royal carriage came along a little later, the King, taking an interest in everything he saw, did not fail to ask the mowers whose field they were mowing, as the cat had guessed he would.

'It belongs to Monsieur le Marquis de Carabas,' they chorused all together, for the cat's threat had frightened them considerably.

'You have a fine inheritance there,' said the King to the Marquis de Carabas.

'As you see, Sire,' the Marquis replied, thinking fast. 'It is a meadow which never fails to crop heavily every year.'

Next the Master Cat, still going on ahead, met with some harvesters, and he spoke to them in the same fashion, saying:

'Good harvesters, if you do not say that all these wheat fields belong to Monsieur le Marquis de Carabas, you will all be chopped up as fine as meat for a pâté.'

Naturally the King, passing by a moment later, wanted to know who owned all the fields he saw.

'It is Monsieur le Marquis de Carabas,' replied the harvesters, and the King once again rejoiced with the Marquis in his good fortune.

Meanwhile the cat, who always went on ahead of the carriage, said the same thing to everyone he met, and the

King was astonished by the huge wealth of Monsieur le Marquis de Carabas.

At last the Master Cat arrived at a magnificent castle, the lord of which was an ogre, the richest ever known, for all the lands through which the King had been driving, were part of the estate belonging to his castle. The cat had taken care to find out about this ogre, and knew what he must do. He asked to speak with him, saying that he had not wanted to pass so close to his castle without having the honour of paying his respects.

The ogre received him as courteously as an ogre can, and invited him to sit down.

'I have been very credibly informed,' said the cat, 'that you have the gift of being able to change yourself into all sorts of animals; that you could, for example, transform yourself into a lion, say, or an elephant . . .'

'That is correct,' the ogre replied brusquely. 'And to prove it, I'll turn myself into a lion for you.'

The cat was so terrified to see a lion standing before him, that he made a leap for the roof and reached the gutters in no time, but not without some difficulty and danger, because his boots were not much good for walking on the tiles.

Some time later, when he saw that the ogre had divested himself of his first alarming disguise, the cat came down and confessed that he had been very much afraid. (Which rather pleased the ogre.)

'Another thing I was told,' said the cat, 'although I don't see how it could be true, was that you also have the power to take the shape of the smallest animals, to change yourself into a rat or a mouse, for instance. I have to confess that I find that quite impossible to believe.'

'Impossible?' exclaimed the ogre. 'Well, you shall see!'

And in the same instant he changed himself into a mouse, which started to run across the floor. The cat had no sooner seen him, than he leapt down and ate him.

Meanwhile the King had seen the ogre's handsome castle

in passing, and wanted to go in. Hearing the noise of the carriage crossing the drawbridge, the cat ran to meet it, and said to the King:

'Your Majesty, welcome to the castle of Monsieur le Marquis de Carabas!'

'What, Monsieur le Marquis?' cried the King. 'This castle is yours too? I've never seen anything finer than this courtyard and all the buildings around it. Please let us see inside.'

The Marquis gave his hand to the young Princess, and following the King, who went up first, they entered a great banqueting hall, where they found already set out a magnificent meal, prepared by the ogre for his friends, who should have been coming to see him that very day, but who had not dared to when they knew that the King was there.

The King was charmed by the excellent qualities of the Marquis de Carabas almost as much as his daughter, who was perfectly silly about them, and seeing what great wealth he possessed, he said to him, after drinking five or six glasses of wine:

'There's no reason, Monsieur le Marquis, why you shouldn't be my son-in-law, if you choose.'

The Marquis, bowing deeply, accepted the honour the King did him, and he married the Princess that very day!

The cat became a great lord, and no longer ran after mice, except to amuse himself.

Dear Madame,

*   You describe your life as 'a dull provincial existence', yet you make it sound so attractive, I wonder how you will bring yourself to change it for Paris again. I feel I have become as well acquainted with your neighbours and their little oddities, as if I had met them myself. I picture you walking in your beautiful woodlands, and now that spring is really with us at last, I cannot imagine anything more delightful.*

*   I am vastly relieved to learn that Mademoiselle is not yet so grown up as to despise the nursery tales I send her. You say she beseeches me to forgive her for teasing – but what is there to forgive? So she sharpens her young wit on an old friend? Well, I am glad to be such a friend.*

*   But no sooner have you reassured me, than you cast me down again. You tell me that my stories are acceptable to your daughter – and then find fault yourself with the morals I draw from them. You point out that I have claimed that my story of the Master Cat recommends talent, application and ingenuity, but whose talent, application and ingenuity, you exclaim? If my moral is to run true, surely the cat should have the Princess?*

*   What defence can I offer to such penetrating criticism? I can only suggest another moral, which you may find more convincing than my first. If a miller's son can win the heart of a princess so quickly, and become the object of her*

35

languishing gaze, it may be because fine clothes, good looks and youth are by no means the worst ways of inspiring affection. (Ah, but I will not let you draw me with your remarks about self-made noblemen, who pop up overnight, or your wicked speculations as to whether you might actually have met the Marquis de Carabas and his so admirably well-informed servant. I insist that it is a fairytale, no more, and I will not be held responsible for what anyone else may read into it!)

But now, lest you accuse me again of worldliness, I shall seek to save my credit by suggesting a moral for the little tale I send today, before you and Mademoiselle have a chance to analyse it to death.

It is that gentle words are of greater price than diamonds and gold pieces, and have greater power to sway minds. Furthermore, that though courtesy costs some thought and care, and it may be necessary to put oneself out a little for it, yet sooner or later it will be rewarded, and often just when one is least expecting a reward . . .

The Fairy Gifts

THERE was once a widow who had two daughters, the elder of whom resembled her so strongly in appearance and character that whoever looked at her saw the mother, and they were both so proud and disagreeable, that there was no living with either of them. The younger, who was the very image of her father for kindness and courtesy, was also one of the most beautiful girls one could hope to see, but since like is naturally drawn to like, the mother doted on her elder daughter, while at the same time displaying a frightful aversion for the younger. She made her eat in the kitchen and work unceasingly.

Among all her other duties this poor child was

obliged to go twice a day to draw water from a spring a good half league from home, and bring back a great pitcher full right up to the top. One day when she was at the fountain, a poor old woman came up to her and begged a drink.

'But of course, good mother,' said the beautiful girl, and immediately rinsing her pitcher, she drew some water from the clearest part of the spring, and offered it to her, supporting the pitcher all the while, so that she could drink more comfortably.

When she had drunk her fill, the goodwife said:

'You are so beautiful, so good and so well-mannered, that I cannot forbear giving you a gift.' (For this was a Fay, who had taken the guise of a poor countrywoman, in order to find out how far the young girl's courtesy went.) 'I give you the gift,' the Fay continued, 'that at every word you speak, a flower or a precious stone will fall from your mouth.'

When the lovely girl arrived home, her mother scolded her for returning so late from the spring.

'I beg your pardon for having loitered so long, Mother,' said the poor girl, and as she uttered these words, two roses, two pearls and two enormous diamonds fell from her mouth.

'What's that I see?' said her mother in astonishment. 'I thought I saw pearls and diamonds coming out of her mouth. How has this come about, Daughter?' (This was the first time she had ever called her Daughter.)

The poor child innocently told her all that had happened to her, not without spilling a wealth of diamonds.

'Indeed,' said the mother. 'I must send my elder daughter there. Come here, Fanchon, look what comes out of your sister's mouth, when she speaks. Wouldn't you be glad to have the same gift? You only have to go and draw water at the spring, and when a poor woman asks you for a drink, give it to her politely.'

'It'd be a fine thing for *me* to go to the spring!' the ill-mannered creature replied.

'I want you to go,' snapped her mother. 'And right away!'

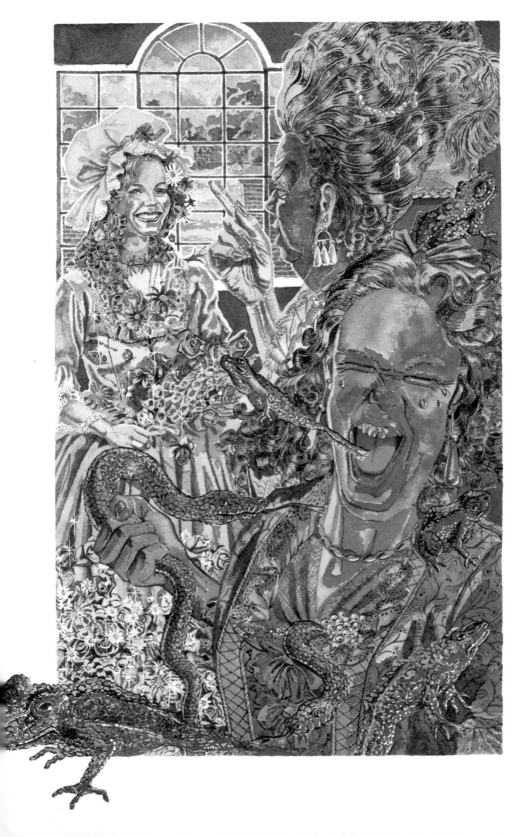

In the end she went, but grumbling all the way and taking the finest silver flagon in the house. She had no sooner arrived at the spring, than she saw coming out of the wood a magnificently dressed lady, who asked her for a drink. This was the same Fay who had appeared to her sister, but this time she had adopted the clothes and manners of a princess to see how far the discourtesy of this girl would go.

'Do you think I've come here just to give you a drink?' said this vulgar, conceited slut. 'Is it likely that I'd have brought a silver flagon especially to give a drink to Madame? I should think so! Drink from the spring, if you want to.'

'That's hardly very polite,' said the Fay, without losing her temper. 'Well, since you are so disobliging, I give you for a gift that at every word you speak a serpent or a toad shall fall from your mouth.'

As soon as her mother saw her she called to her:

'Well, Daughter?'

'Well what, Mother?' replied the rude girl, spitting out two vipers and two toads.

'Heavens above!' cried the mother. 'What's this I see? Her sister is at the bottom of this. She shall answer to me for it.' And she ran in at once and began to beat the younger girl.

When the poor child managed to escape from her, she fled for her life into the nearby forest, where it happened that the King's son, who was returning from the hunt, met her. Seeing how beautiful she was, he asked her what she was doing there all alone, and what she had to cry about.

'Alas Sir, my mother has driven me away from home,' she said.

Seeing five or six pearls and as many diamonds fall from her mouth, the King's son begged her to tell him how this came about, and she recounted all her adventure to him. Even as she spoke, the King's son fell in love with her, and considering that such a gift was worth more than all that might be given as a dowry if he married another, he took her to the palace of the King his father, where he married her.

As for her sister, she made herself so obnoxious, that her own mother drove her out of the house. After running a long way without finding anyone who was prepared to take her in, the unhappy girl died in a corner of the forest.

Dear Madame,

Your repeated assurances that my tales are well received,
by yourself no less than my little Mademoiselle, give me great
encouragement. You see, there are would-be serious persons,
with just enough wit to see that fairytales are made to please
and that their subject matter has no great weight, who regard
them with contempt. It is very satisfying, therefore, to find
that people of good taste pass a different judgement on them.

You have been pleased to note, that though these stories
are trifles, they are not merely trifles. There is always some
useful lesson contained in them. You might think that would
be enough to clear me of the charge of wasting my time on
frivolities. However, I have dealings with a good many folk,
who are not satisfied with plain sense, but are guided only by
the authority and example of the Ancients, and so I am
obliged to prepare a stronger defence.

So let us consider the Ancients. What do we find? That
the fables which delighted Athens and Rome were of just the
same sort as these of mine! And think of some of the other
celebrated stories of antiquity: 'The Matron of Ephesus', for
instance; is that not a novella like 'Griselidis'? That is to say,
they both tell of things which could happen, and which do not
utterly violate probability. Then there is the 'Tale of Psyche',
which is the purest fiction – every bit as much a fairytale as
'Donkeyskin'. Look at the 'Fable of the Ploughman', who

obtained from Jupiter the power to make it rain or shine when he pleased, but used it in such a way that he harvested nothing but straw without grain, because he had never asked for wind or cold or snow, all of which are necessary to make plants fruitful. I tell you, this fable is near kin to 'The Ridiculous Wishes'. The one is serious, the other comic, nevertheless both teach that men do not know what is good for them, and that they are happier when their affairs are in the hands of Providence, than if everything were to be arranged according to their wishes.

Since I have set such fine models before me, drawn from the wisest, most learned Antiquity, I do not believe that anyone has the right to reproach me in any way.

I am prepared to go further. I am even prepared to claim that my fables are in fact more worthy of repetition than most of the classical tales, if you consider the morals to be drawn from them. This, after all, is the main point of fables, the purpose for which they are framed. Yet all the moral you can draw from 'The Matron of Ephesus', is that those women who seem most virtuous are often least so, and so there are almost none who really are. Now it must be obvious that this is a very bad moral; one that can only corrupt women by bad example and make them believe, that by failing in their duty, they do no more than follow the common way of the world. 'Griselidis', on the other hand, teaches that the patience of a good woman is invincible, no matter how rude and strange the behaviour of her husband.

As for the 'Tale of Psyche', a very agreeable and ingenious story in itself I grant you – well, I would compare its moral with that of 'Donkeyskin', if I knew how, but so far I have not been able to work out what it is. I know Psyche is supposed to represent the soul, but I do not understand what Cupid represents in this, and even less why Psyche should be happy when she does not know who loves her – that is to say Cupid, or Love himself – but is very unhappy the moment she does know. I rather think it shows, that the Ancients frequently indulged in the frivolous practice of telling stories for no purpose but pleasure, with scant regard for morality, which they neglected considerably.

The same certainly cannot be said of the tales our ancestors invented for their children. They did not tell them with classical elegance, or embellish them as the Greeks and Romans did their fables, but they always took great care that their stories should contain a commendable and instructive lesson. Virtue is always rewarded and vice is punished. They all demonstrate the advantages of being mannerly, patient, prudent, hardworking and obedient, and the evil which befalls those who scorn these things.

However frivolous and fantastic the adventures in these tales, they certainly inspire in children a desire to be like those, whom they see achieve happiness, and at the same time a fear of those misfortunes into which the wicked fall through their wickedness. Is it not commendable, that when their children are still too young to relish solid truth unadorned, parents will coax them to swallow such nourishment, by serving it up in amusing narratives suited to the tenderness of their years? It is hardly credible how avidly these innocent souls, in whom nothing has yet corrupted a natural sense of what is right, receive this hidden teaching. You see them sad and dejected as long as the hero or heroine of the tale is suffering misfortune, and exclaiming with joy, when the hour of their triumph arrives. These seeds, which at first produce only the stirrings of joy and sorrow, can hardly fail to bloom as inclinations to good.

My dear Madame, what a sermon I have written you on the subject of fairytales! You see how dangerous it is to challenge my seriousness.

And my other charming correspondent will be imagining by now that I am so taken up with theorising about stories, that I shall have no time to tell one. I must set her mind at rest immediately. After such a dry dissertation, I can only offer one of the prettiest tales I know . . .

The Little Glass Slipper

THERE was once a gentleman, who marrying for a
second time, took as his wife the proudest, haugh-
tiest woman you ever saw. She had two daughters
who resembled her in temperament, and indeed in
every other respect. For his part the husband also
had a young daughter, but no one was kinder or
gentler than she, and in this she took after her
mother, who had been the best woman in the
world.

The wedding was no sooner over, than the
stepmother began to display her evil temper. She
could not abide the good qualities of her husband's
child, for they made her own daughters look still
more detestable. Accordingly she set her to do all

the unpleasantest housework: it was she who washed the dishes and cleaned the stairs, she who swept Madame's room and those of Mesdemoiselles her daughters. She herself slept in an attic at the top of the house, on a wretched straw mattress, while her step-sisters had rooms with polished floors, beds with elegant new hangings and mirrors in which they could see themselves from head to foot. The poor girl endured it all patiently, not daring to complain to her father, who would only have scolded her, because his wife dominated him completely.

When she had finished her work, she used to go and tuck herself away in the inglenook to sit among the cinders, as a result of which she was commonly known around the house as Cinderbum, but her younger stepsister, who was not as ill-mannered as the elder, called her Little Cinders. All the same, Little Cinders in her miserable rags could not help being a hundred times more beautiful than her sisters, however magnificently they dressed.

Now it happened that the King's son was to give a ball, to which he had invited all the nobility, and our two young ladies were invited as well, for they cut a fine figure in Society. There they were, very happy and busy choosing the clothes and hairstyles which would suit them best – all of which only made more trouble for Little Cinders, of course, since it was she who ironed her sisters' linen and pleated their cuffs. They talked of nothing but how they were going to get themselves up for the occasion.

'I shall wear my red velvet gown,' said the elder. 'With my English accessories.'

'I've only got my old skirt,' said the younger. 'But to make up for that I'll wear my gold-flowered mantle and my diamond stomacher, which isn't at all bad.'

They sent out to find a good hairdresser to put up their hair in elaborate arrangements of curls, and they bought velvet patches for their faces from the best maker. They called Little Cinders in to ask her opinion, for she had very good taste, and she gave them the best advice they could have had. She even offered to do their hair herself, which they accepted gladly.

While she was dressing their hair, they said to her:

'Cinders, would you like to go to the ball?'

'Oh dear,' said Little Cinders. 'You're mocking me, Mesdemoiselles. That's not the place for me.'

'You're right,' they said. 'People would certainly laugh to see a little Cinderbum going to the ball!'

Anyone but Little Cinders would have put their hair up all askew for that, but she was a good girl and did it perfectly.

Altogether the two step-sisters were so beside themselves with joy that they went for nearly two days without eating. They had broken more than a dozen corset laces through pulling them too tight in order to make their waists tinier, and they were forever parading in front of their mirrors.

At last the happy day arrived, and Little Cinders stood at the window following them with her eyes until they were out of sight. When she could see them no more, she sat down and cried.

And that was how her godmother found her a little later, all in tears. She asked her what was the matter.

'I wish . . . I do so wish . . .' She was crying so hard she could not get the words out.

Her godmother, who was a Fay, said:

'You'd very much like to go to the ball, that's the trouble, isn't it?'

'Oh dear, yes,' said Cinders, sighing.

'Well now,' said her godmother. 'If you promise to be a good girl, I'll see that you go.'

She took her into her own room and said:

'Go into the garden and fetch me a pumpkin.'

Cinders could not imagine how a pumpkin could help her go to the ball, but she went at once and cut the best she could find, and took it to her godmother, who set to work hollowing it out. When only the rind was left, she tapped it with her ring, and the pumpkin was at once changed into a beautiful carriage, gilded all over.

Then she went to her mousetrap, where she found six mice, all alive. She told Cinders to lift the door of the trap a little, and as each mouse came out, she gave it a tap with her ring, and the mouse was at once changed into a fine horse, which made a handsome team of six beautiful dappled greys (a little mousey in colour).

She was hard put then to think what to do for a coachman, but Cinders, who was beginning to enter into the spirit of the game, said:

'I'll go and see if there isn't a rat in the rat trap. If there is, we could make a coachman out of that.'

'You're right,' said her godmother. 'Go and see.'

Cinders brought her the rat trap, in which there were three fat rats. The Fay picked one of them on account of his imposing whiskers, and when she touched him, he was changed into a stout coachman, who had the most splendid moustache you ever saw.

Then she said:

'Go into the garden again. You'll find six lizards behind the watering can. Bring them to me.'

The moment she brought them in, her godmother changed them into six footmen, who straightway jumped up behind the carriage in their gold braided coats, and hung on there as if they had never done anything else all their lives.

Then the Fay said to Little Cinders:

'Well, there's all you need to go to the ball. Aren't you pleased?'

'Yes,' said Cinders uncertainly. 'But am I to go like this, in my shabby old clothes?'

Her godmother did no more than touch her with her ring, and in that same instant her clothes were transformed into a gown of gold and silver tissue all encrusted with precious stones. Finally she gave her a pair of glass slippers, the prettiest in the world.

When she was thus gorgeously arrayed, Little Cinders stepped up into the carriage, but before allowing her to depart her godmother warned her above all things to be sure not to stay out after midnight, because if she lingered at the ball a moment more her carriage would become a pumpkin once more, her horses mice, her footmen lizards, and her old clothes would revert to their original condition.

Cinders promised that she would not fail to leave before midnight, and drove off dazed with joy.

At the palace the King's son was warned that a great princess, whom no one knew at all, had just arrived, and he ran to receive her. He handed her down from her carriage and led her into the ballroom, where the company was gathered. A great silence fell; people stopped dancing and the violins played no more, they were all so rapt in contemplation of the dazzling charms of the unknown lady. Then a low, confused sound was heard, as people whispered: 'Ah, how beautiful she is!' The King himself, old as he was, could not stop looking at her, murmuring to the Queen that it was a long time since he had seen such a beautiful and gracious creature. All the ladies studied her hair and clothes closely, so as to be able to order the same for themselves first thing next morning, providing there were materials as luxurious and workers as skilful to be found.

The King's son seated her in the place of honour, then later took her hand to lead her in the dance, and she danced with such grace, that everyone marvelled at it all over again.

A splendid supper was served, of which the young Prince did not eat a mouthful, he was so busy watching her every move. She went and sat next to her sisters and offered them a thousand civilities, even sharing with them the oranges and lemons, which the Prince had given her. This astonished them greatly, for they did not recognise her at all.

While they were chatting like this, Little Cinders heard

the clock strike a quarter to twelve. She made a deep curtsey to the company and took herself off as quickly as she could.

As soon as she arrived home, she went to find her godmother, and after thanking her, she told her that she would very much like to go to another ball the following evening, to which the King's son had invited her. As she was busy telling her godmother all that had happened at the ball, the two sisters knocked at the door. Cinders went and opened it to them.

'What an age you've been gone!' she said, yawning, rubbing her eyes and stretching, as if she had only just woken up (though she had not had the least inclination to sleep, since they had gone out).

'If you had come to the ball, you wouldn't have been so bored there,' said one of her sisters. 'The most beautiful princess turned up – the most beautiful anyone had ever seen. She was so gracious to us – she gave us oranges and lemons!'

Cinders nearly choked with delight. She asked them the name of this princess, but they replied that no one had known her, that the Prince was distracted, and that he would give everything in the world to find out who she was.

Cinders smiled and said:

'She was so beautiful, then? Goodness, how lucky you are. Isn't there any way I could see her? Oh dear, lend me your yellow gown, Mademoiselle Javotte – the one you wear for everyday.'

'Indeed!' said Mademoiselle Javotte. 'Lend a gown to a wretched Cinderbum like you? I should think so! I'd need to be crazy.'

Cinders expected this refusal, and she was very glad of it, for she would have been greatly embarrassed, if her sister had been quite willing to lend the gown.

The next evening the two sisters went to the ball again, and so did Little Cinders, but even more brilliantly dressed than the first time.

The King's son was always at her side, and never stopped

saying the most delightful things to her. The young lady did not find this at all boring, so much so that she quite forgot her godmother's warning, and was horrified to hear the first stroke of midnight, when she thought it could not possibly be more than eleven o'clock. She jumped up and fled from the ballroom as swiftly and lightly as a deer. The Prince ran after her, but he could not catch up with her. As she ran, however, she dropped one of her glass slippers, which he found and picked up with the greatest care.

Little Cinders arrived home all out of breath, without coach or footmen and wearing her wretched old clothes. Nothing remained of all her glorious finery but one of her little slippers, the fellow of the one she had dropped.

Meanwhile the guards at the palace gate were questioned as to whether they had seen anything of a princess departing in haste, to which they replied that they had seen no one leave except a girl in rags, who looked more like a peasant than a fine young lady.

When her two sisters returned from the ball, Little Cinders asked if they had enjoyed themselves again, and if the beautiful lady had been there. They said that she had, but that she had run away on the stroke of midnight, so quickly that she had dropped one of her glass slippers, the prettiest thing in the world, which the Prince had picked up. They added that since he had done nothing but look at it for the rest of the ball, it was certain that he must be very much in love with the enchanting creature to whom the little slipper belonged.

What they said was no more than the truth, for a few days later the King's son had it announced with a fanfare of trumpets, that he would marry the woman whose foot the slipper fitted exactly. First the princesses were tried, then the duchesses and all the court, but it was useless. Eventually it was carried to the home of the two sisters. They did everything they could to force their feet into it, but came nowhere near succeeding.

Little Cinders, who was watching them and who naturally recognised her own slipper, said laughing:

'How I should like to see if it wouldn't suit me nicely!'

Her sisters started to laugh and to mock her, but the gentleman who was in charge of the slipper, having looked closely at Little Cinders and finding her very beautiful, said that this was reasonable, for he had been ordered to try it on all the girls in the kingdom. He sat Cinders down, and presenting the slipper to her little foot, he saw that it went on without difficulty; indeed it fitted as if it had been made to her measure.

The astonishment of the two sisters was enormous, but it became even greater when Little Cinders pulled from her pocket the other slipper, which she put on her other foot. Thereupon the godmother entered, and with a touch of her ring transformed Cinders' clothes into a costume still more magnificent than the others.

At that her two sisters recognised her as the beautiful lady they had seen at the ball. They fell at her feet to beg her pardon for all the ill treatment they had made her suffer, but Cinders lifted them up, and said embracing them, that she forgave them with all her heart, and begged them always to love her.

She was taken to the young Prince in all the splendour of her fairy gown. He found her more beautiful than ever, and a few days later he married her. Little Cinders, who was as good as she was beautiful, took her sisters to live with her in the palace, and arranged for them to be married on the same day to two great lords of the Court.

Dear Madame,

You are quite right: after all my solemn rigmarole about morals, I overlooked one for Little Cinders. Yet do I need to moralise this tale for such a daughter of such a mother? Perhaps since you are both so modest, I must spell it out.

Beauty is a rare treasure, which never fails to be admired, but grace and kindness are beyond price. Yet alas, the world being what it is, I can now see another possible moral. It is no doubt a great advantage to have beauty and charm, as well as all the other gifts of that sort, but none of them will do you the slightest good, if you do not have influential godparents to help you make the most of them!

Your other comment on Little Cinders came as something of a surprise to me. I suppose it is true: the heroines of most fairytales are indeed beautiful, and now you mention it, I will concede that their good qualities could be said to be – well, a little passive, perhaps, though I cannot altogether agree with your use of the word 'insipid'. You ask me what hope the majority of girls, who are not dazzlingly beautiful, may glean from such stories. You further suggest that it is a large defect in the morality of fairytales, that they appear to allow for no wit in womankind – no virtues at all, save meekness.

Madame, I think I have here the very story to satisfy your criticisms. And the moral? That all is beautiful which is loved, and all that is loved is witty!

Riquet the Tuft

THERE was once a Queen, who was brought to bed of a son so ugly and so misshapen, that it seemed doubtful for some time whether he were quite human. However, a Fay who was present at the birth declared that, whatever his appearance, he could not fail to be attractive, because he would have plenty of wit and intelligence. She even added that by virtue of the gift she meant to give him, he would be able to give as much intelligence as he had himself, to the person he loved best.

All this consoled the poor Queen a little, for she was very distressed to have brought such an ugly little monkey into the world, and sure enough the child had no sooner started to speak, than he said a thousand pretty things. In all his actions too there was something so indefinably witty, that everyone found him quite charming. (I forgot to say that he came into the world with a little tuft of hair on his head, which led to him being called Riquet the Tuft, Riquet being the family's name.)

Seven or eight years later the Queen of a neighbouring realm gave birth to two daughters. The first to come into the world was more beautiful than the day, and the Queen was so delighted with her, that the people around her were concerned lest this excess of joy should actually be harmful to her. The same Fay who had attended the birth of little Riquet the Tuft, was present at this one, and to bring the Queen down to earth, she announced that this baby princess would not have the least intelligence, in fact she would be as stupid as she was beautiful. The Queen was deeply mortified at this, but a few moments later she had an even greater vexation, for the second daughter she bore was extremely ugly.

'There is no need to be so distressed, Madame,' said the Fay. 'Your daughter will be compensated in another respect: she will have so much intelligence, that her lack of beauty will hardly be noticed.'

'So be it,' sighed the Queen. 'But wouldn't there be some way of giving just a little wit to the elder, since she's so beautiful.'

'As far as wits are concerned, Madame, I can do nothing for her,' said the Fay firmly. 'But I can do something more in the matter of beauty. As there is nothing I'm prepared to do to satisfy your wishes, I am going to give her as a gift the power to make beautiful anyone she pleases.'

As these two princesses grew up, so their particular gifts grew with them, and people everywhere spoke of nothing but the beauty of the elder and the cleverness of the younger. However, it is also true that their faults increased greatly with the years as well. The younger grew visibly uglier, and the elder became more stupid from day to day – either she made no reply to anything she was asked, or she said

something abysmally silly. In addition to this she was so clumsy, that she could not arrange four china ornaments on a mantelpiece without breaking one of them, nor drink a glass of water without spilling half of it down her clothes.

Although beauty may be a great advantage in a young person, nevertheless the younger girl almost always had the better of her elder sister in any company. At first people would be drawn to the more beautiful princess, simply for the sake of looking at her and admiring her, but very soon they drifted away to the one who had more intelligence, for the sake of her pleasant, witty conversation. It was quite astonishing, how within less than a quarter of an hour there was no one left near the elder, and everyone was gathered round the younger.

Stupid as she was, the elder was well aware of what happened and why, and she would have given all her beauty without a moment's regret, to have had half her sister's intelligence. Even the Queen, an admirably sensible woman, could not resist reproaching her at times for her stupidity, which made the poor princess so unhappy she almost wished herself dead.

One day when she had retreated into a wood to be miserable over her misfortune in peace, she saw a little man approaching her, very ugly and very unattractive, but very magnificently dressed. This was the young Prince Riquet the Tuft, who, having fallen in love with her from her portraits, which were spread throughout the world, had left his father's kingdom so that he might have the pleasure of seeing and speaking with her. Delighted to meet her alone in this way, he addressed himself to her with all the respect and courtesy imaginable. But after paying her all the conventional compliments, he noticed that she was very melancholy, and said:

'I do not understand, Madame, how anyone as beautiful as you undoubtedly are, should be as sad as you seem; for though I can boast of having seen an infinity of lovely women, I can truly say that I have never seen one whose beauty approaches yours.'

'It pleases you to say so, Monsieur,' replied the Princess, and very sensibly left it at that.

'Beauty,' continued Riquet the Tuft, 'is so great an advantage, that it must take precedence of all the rest, and when one possesses it, I do not see that there is anything which could greatly distress one.'

'I would rather be as ugly as you and be clever,' said the Princess, 'than to have beauty such as I have and be as stupid as I am.'

'There is nothing, Madame,' said Riquet, 'which shows more clearly that one has intelligence, than to believe that one has not, and it is the nature of that gift, that the more one has it, the more one believes oneself to lack it.'

'I don't know about that,' said the Princess. 'But I do know very well that I'm extremely stupid, and that's why I'm so miserable I could die.'

'If that's all that's distressing you, Madame, I can easily put an end to your unhappiness,' said the Prince.

'And how will you do that?' said the Princess.

'Madame,' said Riquet the Tuft, 'I have the power to give as much intelligence as you can imagine to the person I love best. As you, Madame, are that person, there's no reason why you should not have as much intelligence as it's possible to have, providing you are willing to marry me.'

The Princess was completely taken aback, and made no reply.

'I see,' continued Riquet the Tuft, 'that this proposal has disturbed you, and I am not surprised, but I will give you a whole year to think about it.'

The Princess had so little intelligence, and at the same time such a great desire for it, that the end of the year seemed to her so far away that it might never come, and so she accepted the Prince's proposal.

She had no sooner promised Riquet the Tuft that she

would marry him on that same day the following year, than she felt altogether different: it was quite unlike she had ever felt before. Suddenly she found it incredibly easy to say everything she wanted, and moreover to say it precisely, effortlessly and naturally. She at once began an elegant and sustained conversation with Riquet, in which she shone so brilliantly, that he began to believe he had given her more intelligence than he had kept for himself.

When she returned to the palace, no one at Court knew what to think of such a sudden and extraordinary change, for she talked as much sense now as she had talked nonsense before, and she was heard to say things which were not only well judged but infinitely witty. The whole Court was more pleased by this change than you could imagine – only the younger princess was not entirely happy, because no longer having the advantage of intelligence over her elder sister, she seemed merely apishly unattractive beside her.

The King was guided by the elder's advice, and some-times even held meetings of his Council in her apartment.

News of this transformation being spread abroad, all the young princes of the neighbouring kingdoms did whatever they could to win her approval, and almost all asked for her hand in marriage; but none of them was clever enough for her, and she listened to them all without becoming attached to any one of them. However, there came a prince at last, who was so powerful, so rich, so intelligent and so handsome, that she could not help being attracted to him. Having become aware of this, her father told her that she should be her own mistress in the choice of a husband, and that she had only to declare her wishes.

The greater one's intelligence, the greater the difficulty one is likely to experience in coming to a firm decision on a matter such as this, and so, after thanking her father, she asked him to give her time to think about it.

It so happened that in order to think over quietly what she should do, she went for a walk in the same wood where she had met Riquet the Tuft. While she was walking there deep in thought, she heard a muffled sound under her feet, such as might be made by a number of people bustling back and forth. Giving a more attentive ear to what was going on, she found she could hear what they were saying.

'Bring me that pot,' said one voice.

'Give me that copper pan,' said another.

'Put some wood on the fire,' said a third.

At the same moment the earth opened before her, and she saw at her feet a vast kitchen, full of cooks, scullions and every other sort of person necessary to create a magnificent banquet. There emerged from this cave a band of twenty or thirty rotisseurs, who went and camped in an avenue of trees around a very long table, where they all set to, larding skewer in hand and fox's tail behind the ear, and began to work to the strains of a harmonious song.

Astonished by this spectacle, the Princess asked them for whom they worked.

'Madame,' replied the most important-looking individual in the group. 'We work for Prince Riquet the Tuft, whose wedding is to take place tomorrow.'

Then the Princess was more surprised than ever. She suddenly remembered that it was a year to the day, since she had promised to marry Riquet the Tuft, and nearly collapsed on the spot. (The reason why she had not remembered this before, was that when she had made the promise she was still a fool, but when the Prince had given her the new mind, she had forgotten all her former foolishness.)

She continued her walk, but she had not taken more than another thirty paces, when Riquet the Tuft presented himself before her, elegant, magnificent and every inch a prince about to be married.

'Here I am, Madame,' he said. 'Punctual according to my word, and I have not the least doubt that you have come here to keep yours, and make me the happiest of men by giving me your hand.'

'I freely confess,' replied the Princess, 'that I have not yet made up my mind on that matter, and that I do not believe I shall ever be able to decide it in the way you wish.'

'You astonish me, Madame,' said Riquet the Tuft.

'I believe you,' said the Princess. 'And assuredly if I were dealing with an uncivilised man, a man without intelligence or any finer feelings, I should find myself in a most embarrassing situation—a princess has only her word, he would say, and you must marry me, since you promised it. But since the man to whom I am speaking is in fact the most intelligent in the world, I am sure he will hear reason. You know that even when I was a fool, I could not make up my mind to marry you. The intelligence you gave me has made me even more cautious about people than I was, so how can you expect me to be able to make today a decision I could not make then? If you seriously thought to marry me, you made a great mistake in relieving me of my stupidity, and making me see more clearly what I did not see before.'

'If a man without intelligence would be justified, as you have just said, in reproaching you for breaking your word, why, Madame, do you expect me not to do the same, in a matter which concerns all the happiness of my life?' replied Riquet the Tuft. 'Is it reasonable that those who have intelligence should be worse off than those who do not? Can you truly assert this, you who have so much, and who so much desired to have it? But let us come to the real point, please. Apart from my ugliness, is there anything about me which displeases you; are you dissatisfied with my birth, my intelligence, my character or my manners?'

'Nothing at all,' replied the Princess. 'I like everything in you that you have just mentioned.'

'If that is so,' Riquet continued, 'I am going to be lucky, for you are able to make me the most attractive of men.'

'How can that be done?' asked the Princess.

'It will be done,' said Riquet, 'if you love me enough to wish that it may be. If you have any doubts, Madame, you should know that the same Fay, who on the day of my birth made me a gift of the power to make any person I pleased intelligent, also gave you the power to make beautiful whoever you loved, and on whom you truly wished to bestow this favour.'

'If that is the case,' said the Princess, 'I wish with all my heart that you should become the handsomest and most attractive prince in the world, and I gladly give you as much of this gift as I have it in my power to give.'

The Princess had no sooner pronounced these words, than Riquet the Tuft appeared to her eyes the most handsome man in the world, the finest and most charming that she had ever seen.

Now, some people say that this had nothing whatsoever to do with the workings of the Fay's spells, but that love alone accomplished this metamorphosis. They say that the Princess, having reflected on her lover's perseverance, on his discretion, and on all his other good qualities of mind and spirit, no longer saw the deformity of his body, nor the ugliness of his face. They say that his hunched back seemed to her no more than the easy manner of a man who shrugs his shoulders, and that whereas until then she had seen him limp frightfully, she now found in him no more than a certain leaning stance, which quite charmed her. They say furthermore that his squinting eyes only shone the more brilliantly in her sight, since their misalignment passed in her mind for the indication of a violent excess of love, and finally that for her his huge red nose had something warlike and heroic about it!

Whatever the truth of the matter, the Princess promised on the spot to marry him, providing he obtained the consent of the King her father. The King, knowing already that his daughter esteemed Riquet the Tuft, whom he knew from other sources to be a very wise and prudent prince, received him with pleasure as his son-in-law. The wedding took place early next day, even as Riquet had foreseen, and according to the orders he had given long beforehand.

Dear Madame,

You are hard taskmistresses. It is the beautiful girl who comes out best again, you point out, and my little Mademoiselle is anxious about the future of the ugly girl. Well, perhaps once her sister was out of the way, she was able to shine again herself. Do you not think that very likely? Perhaps she married the poor man the elder abandoned, when she renewed her promise to Riquet. Indeed, now I give a little more thought to the matter, I am sure that must have been the way of it. Yes and maybe you are both right about Prince Riquet and his Princess. They do sound like a terribly precious pair, always ready to turn the simplest thing into a philosophical debate or an opera.

So there, you have as good as proved that Princess Uglymug had the best of it in the end anyway!

Nevertheless, I still insist on my moral. Let me try to put it better this time. Nature may produce a perfect creature—a veritable masterpiece of beauty, with the most delicate features and the most exquisite colouring, such as Art could never aspire to emulate. Yet all this will do less to move a heart to tenderness, than one single invisible charm, which Love causes to be found there.

Yet I sense you do not have much appetite for my trifles just now. You tell me that my view of rural life is too much coloured by poetry, and you write of famine, disease and the threat of a bad harvest. Believe me, I am not unaware of these things. The pitiful tale of your starving peasants is one that may be told of in many parts of the kingdom, in the towns no less than in the countryside. Now we are at war again, I fear conditions can only worsen. It seems it is always the poorest and weakest, who pay the heaviest price for Glory.

However, though you may not have the heart for stories at this time, I know someone who will be expecting another, so let us not disappoint her. Let us try to comfort ourselves with the thought, that it may still be possible to make one's way in the world, with nothing in one's favour but brains.

My story this time is not about princes and princesses, but poor, hard-working people; just such a large, poverty-stricken family, indeed, as those about which you are so concerned.

A large family need be no affliction at all, you know, if they are all good-looking, well grown, healthy and able to make a good showing in the world. If one of them is sickly or tongue-tied, however, he is mocked and despised by all, though it is sometimes this same little monkey, who brings good fortune to the whole family . . .

Little Thummie

THERE was once a woodcutter and his wife, who had seven children, all boys. The eldest was only ten years old and the youngest seven . . .

It was astonishing that the woodcutter had had so many children in so little time but it was because his wife went into labour early and never had less than two at a time . . .

They were very poor, and their seven children made them even poorer, because none of them could yet earn his living. Still more distressing to them, since they took for stupidity what was in fact an indication of the excellence of his mind, was the fact that the youngest was extremely delicate and did not say a word. He was so very small, that when he came into the world, it had been remarked that he seemed hardly fatter than his father's thumb, which was why he was always called Little Thummie.

This poor child was the scapegoat for the entire household, and whatever happened he was always in the wrong. However, he was the shrewdest and most perceptive of the brothers, and if he spoke little, he listened a great deal.

There came a grievous year when the harvest failed, and the famine was so great that these poor people resolved to rid themselves of their children. One evening when the boys were in bed and the woodcutter was sitting at the fireside with his wife, he said to her, his heart crushed with grief:

'You see how it is—we can no longer feed our children, and I can't bear to watch them die of hunger before my eyes, so I've decided to take them to the wood tomorrow and lose them. It'll be quite easy—we only have to slip away without them seeing us, while they are playing at gathering wood.'

'Ah!' cried his wife. 'Could you really, deliberately abandon your own children?'

At first her husband reminded her in vain of their extreme poverty, but whatever he said she could not consent to it. She was poor but she was their mother. However, when she considered what a grief it would be to her to see them starve, she agreed at last, and went to bed weeping.

Little Thummie had heard all they had said. Having heard from his bed that they were talking about family affairs, he had risen quietly and had slid under his father's stool, in order to listen without being seen.

Afterwards he returned to bed, and did not sleep at all for the rest of the night, but lay thinking over what he must do.

Next morning he rose early and went down to the bank of a stream near the house, where he filled his pockets with small white pebbles, and then returned to the house. They set off, and Little Thummie revealed nothing of what he knew to his brothers.

They made their way to a thick forest, where it was

impossible to see another person at a distance of ten paces. The woodcutter set to work felling timber, while his children collected twigs to make faggots. Seeing them busy, the father and mother gradually moved away from them, and then all at once made off along a little footpath, which returned home by a different route.

When the children realised that they were alone, they began to call out for their parents and cry with all their might. Little Thummie let them shout, knowing very well how he would find the way home, for as he had walked along, he had marked the path by dropping the white pebbles he had in his pocket. So he said to his brothers:

'Don't be afraid, Father and Mother have left us here, but I can get you home perfectly well. Just follow me.'

There being nothing else they could do, they followed him, and he led them right to their home on the same path by which they had entered the forest that morning. At first they dared not go in, but put their ears to the door, to hear what their father and mother were saying.

Now, the minute the woodcutter and his wife had returned home, the Lord of the Manor had sent them ten gold pieces, which he had owed them for a long time, and which they had given up any hope of ever seeing again. It had put new life into them, for these poor people were indeed starving. The woodcutter had immediately sent his wife to the butcher's, and since it was a long time since she had last eaten, she had bought three times as much meat as she needed to make supper for two.

When they had eaten their fill, she said:

'Oh dear, where are our poor children now? They would have made a good meal out of what we have left here! But it was you, Guillaume, who wanted to lose them. I said that we'd regret it—I told you so. What are they doing now in that forest? Oh dear! Oh my goodness, perhaps the wolves have eaten them already! You can't be human to have abandoned your children like that.'

The woodcutter lost patience in the end, for she repeated twenty times that she had known that they would regret it, and that she had told him so. He threatened to beat her if she did not keep quiet. It was not that the woodcutter was not as upset as his wife, perhaps even more so, but she was getting on his nerves, and in common with a lot of other people, he claimed to like women who always spoke frankly, but found those who have always 'told you so' very tiresome.

His wife only dissolved in tears, crying all the while:

'Oh dear, oh dear! Where are my children now, my poor little children?'

She cried out so loud, that the children at the door heard her and began to shout all together:

'Here we are, here we are!'

She ran as fast as she could to open the door to them, saying as she embraced them:

'You can't know how glad I am to see you again, my darlings! You must be very tired and hungry. And look how dirty you are, Pierrot; come here while I wash your face.'

(This Pierrot was her eldest son, whom she loved more than all the others, because he was red-haired, and her hair was reddish too.)

They sat down at the table and as they ate, with a hearty appetite which pleased their father and mother, they told them how frightened they had been in the forest—all talking at once most of the time.

The good souls were delighted to see their children home again, and their happiness lasted as long as the ten gold pieces did. When the money was spent, however, they fell back into the same wretchedness as before. Once again they resolved to abandon their children, but this time they intended to take them much further away than they had before, so as not to fail in their plan.

It was impossible for them to discuss this so secretly as to avoid being overheard by Little Thummie, who reckoned he would be able to get out of the situation as he had before. But although he was up good and early the next morning, to go and collect some pebbles, he was unable to do it, for he found the house door locked and barred. It occurred to him, however, when their mother gave each of them a piece of bread for breakfast, that he could use his bread instead of pebbles, by crumbling it and throwing down the crumbs along the paths by which they went, and so he hid it in his pocket.

Their father and mother led them to the thickest, darkest part of the forest, where they left them, returning themselves by a narrow, hidden path. Little Thummie was not greatly upset, because he expected to find the way back quite easily by means of his bread, which he had scattered everywhere he had gone. He was very surprised, therefore, when he could not find a single crumb. The birds had come and eaten it all.

So there they were in a very sad state, for the more they walked, the more lost they became and the deeper they went into the forest. Night came and a great wind rose, which frightened them horribly. On all sides they could hear noises which they took for the howls of wolves coming to eat them. They hardly dared to talk, or even to turn their heads. Then it began to rain heavily, and they were soaked to the bone. They slipped at every step and fell over in the mud, from which they scrambled up all dirty and not knowing what to do with their hands.

Still undaunted, Little Thummie climbed to the top of a tree, to see if he could not find out something that might help them. Scanning the night in all directions he saw at last a tiny glimmer, like that of a candle, but it seemed to be far away beyond the forest. He slid down the tree, eager to tell his good news, but when he reached the ground, he could no longer see anything at all. He was heartbroken. Nevertheless the brothers set off towards the area where he had seen the light, and after walking for some time they saw it again, just as they emerged from the woods.

Even so it was a long time before they arrived at the

house from which this candle was shining out, and they suffered many frights on the way, for they lost sight of it every time they went down into a dip in the ground. At last they stood knocking at the door. The housewife opened it to them and asked what they wanted, and Little Thummie told her that they were poor children, who had lost their way in the forest, begging her to give them a bed for the sake of charity.

Seeing how pretty they all were, the woman began to cry.

'Oh, you poor children!' she said. 'What have you come to? Don't you know that this is the house of an ogre, who eats little children?'

'Oh Madame, what shall we do?' cried Little Thummie, who, like his brothers, was trembling for all he was worth. 'The wolves of the forest will certainly eat us tonight without fail, if you don't give us shelter in your house. And if that's how it's to be, we'd rather it were Monsieur who eats us. Perhaps he might have pity on us, if you were willing to plead on our behalf.'

Thinking she could hide them from her husband until the following morning, the ogre's wife let them in and led them to the fire to warm themselves: it was well stoked up, since there was a whole sheep roasting on the spit for the ogre's supper.

Just as they were beginning to feel warm, they heard three or four loud knocks at the door: the ogre had come home. At once his wife hid them under the bed and went to open the door.

The ogre asked first if supper were ready, and if the wine had been drawn, and straightway sat down at the table. The mutton was still all bloody but that only seemed so much the better to him. Then as he was about to start, he paused and sniffed to right and left, saying that he smelt living flesh.

'It must be that veal I've just dressed, that you can smell,' said his wife.

'I tell you, I can smell living flesh,' repeated the ogre,

looking sideways at his wife. 'And there's something here that I don't understand.'

So saying he stood up from the table and went straight to the bed.

'Damn you, woman! So this is how you try to deceive me!' he exclaimed. 'I can't see why I shouldn't eat you too, only I think you'd be too old and tough. But these little rabbits will do nicely to entertain three ogres of my acquaintance, who will be coming to see me shortly.'

He dragged them one after another from under the bed, and the poor children went down on their knees to beg his pardon. But they were dealing with the cruellest of all ogres, who far from having pity, was already devouring them with his eyes, saying to his wife that they would make a tasty morsel or two, when she served them up in a nice sauce.

He went and got a huge knife, and approached the children, sharpening it on a long stone, which he held in his left hand. He had already grabbed one of them, when his wife said:

'Why do you want to do it at this hour? Won't you have enough time tomorrow morning?'

'Shut up,' said the ogre. 'They'll get tenderer.'

'But you've still got so much meat,' persisted his wife. 'Look—a calf, two sheep and half a pig!'

'You're right,' said the ogre. 'They'll keep. Give them a good supper, so they won't get thin, and put them to bed.'

The good woman was overjoyed and gave them plenty to eat, but they were so overwhelmed with fear, that they could not touch a mouthful. As for the ogre, he sat down again to drink, delighted to have such a delicacy with which to regale his friends. He drank a dozen glasses of wine more than usual, which went to his head somewhat, and he was obliged to go to bed.

Now the ogre had seven daughters, who were still only children. These little ogresses all had a very healthy colour, because they ate fresh meat like their father, and like him they had little round, grey eyes, hooked noses and big mouths with long teeth, very sharp and widely spaced. They were not excessively bad as yet, but they were promising little monsters, for they already bit small children to suck their blood.

They had been put to bed early, and all seven were in one big bed, each with a gold circlet on her head. In the same room there was another bed of the same size, and it was into this bed that the ogre's wife put the seven little boys, after which she went to bed herself beside her husband.

Little Thummie, who feared that the ogre might regret not having cut their throats that same evening, had noticed the gold circlets the ogre's daughters wore. Towards the middle of the night he got up, and taking his brothers' caps and his own, he went very softly to put them on the heads of the ogre's seven daughters, having first relieved them of their crowns, which he put on his brothers' heads and his own, so that the ogre would take them for his daughters, and his daughters for the boys whose throats he wanted to cut.

The trick succeeded as he had anticipated, for the ogre, waking at midnight, regretted having deferred to the morning what he could have done in the evening. Accordingly he jumped out of bed in a hurry, and taking his big knife—

'Let's go and see how our funny little fellows are,' he said. 'And let's make sure we don't have to do it a second time.'

He groped his way up to his daughters' bedroom and approached the bed where the little boys were, all of them asleep except Little Thummie, who was very much afraid, when he felt the ogre's hand pass over his head and the heads of his brothers.

The ogre felt the gold circlets.

''Struth!' he said. 'I was just about to do a pretty piece of work there! I reckon I had too much to drink last night.'

Then he went to his daughters' bed, where he felt the boys' little caps.

'Ah, here they are,' he said. 'Our merry lads! Let's get on with the job and no more messing about.'

So saying he cut the throats of his seven daughters without another thought. Entirely satisfied with his expedition, he went back and lay down beside his wife.

As soon as Little Thummie heard the ogre snoring, he woke his brothers and told them to dress quickly and follow him. They went on tiptoe down into the garden and clambered over the wall, then they ran for almost the whole of the night, shivering with fear all the time and with no idea of where they were going.

On waking up next morning the ogre said to his wife:

'Go up and dress the funny little fellows, who came here last night.'

The ogress was most surprised by her husband's good-nature, not for one moment suspecting that the way he meant her to dress them was as meat, but believing that he was ordering her to go and put their clothes on. She went upstairs, and there she was shocked to see her seven daughters, their throats cut, bathed in their own blood.

The first thing she did was faint (for this is the first expedient, to which almost every woman resorts in circumstances of this sort).

Becoming uneasy at the excessive length of time his wife was taking over the task with which he had charged her, the ogre went up to help her. He was no less astonished than she had been, when he set eyes on the frightful spectacle.

'What have I done?' he cried. 'Those wretches are going to pay for this, as soon as I get my hands on them.'

He straightway threw a pot of water in his wife's face, and having revived her, he said:

'Quick, give me my seven league boots, so that I can go and catch them.'

He set off to search the countryside, and after running great distances in all directions, he happened at last upon the road, along which the poor children were walking. They were by that time no more than a hundred paces from their father's house.

They saw the ogre bounding after them from mountaintop to mountaintop and crossing rivers as easily as he would the smallest stream. Seeing a hollow rock near the place where they were, Little Thummie made his brothers hide there, and then crammed himself in too, looking out all the time to see what became of the ogre.

Very wearied by the long distances he had travelled uselessly (for seven league boots tire their wearer greatly), the ogre wanted to rest, and by chance he sat down and leaned against the rock, where the little boys were hidden.

He was so tired that he could go no further, and after having rested for a while, he fell asleep. Presently he began to snore so frightfully, that the children were no less afraid than when he had fetched his big knife to cut their throats. Little Thummie was not quite as frightened as his brothers, however. He told them to run away home quickly, while the ogre was sound asleep, and said they should not worry about him. They took him at his word and were soon safe at home.

Creeping up to the ogre, Little Thummie cautiously pulled off his boots and put them on himself without delay. The boots were very long and very wide, but being magic they had the property of growing larger or smaller according to the wearer, so that as soon as he put them on they fitted his feet and legs as perfectly as if they had been made for him.

He went straight to the ogre's house, where he found his wife, who was still weeping beside her slaughtered children.

'Your husband is in great danger,' said Little Thummie. 'He has been captured by a band of robbers, who have sworn to kill him, if he doesn't give them all his gold and silver. At the very moment when they were holding him at knife-point, he caught sight of me and begged me to come and warn you of the state he's in, and to tell you to give me everything he owns. You mustn't hold back anything, otherwise they will kill him without mercy. Since the matter is so urgent, he made me take his seven league boots, as you see—both so that I could make haste, and also so that you would not think I was an imposter.'

The good woman was very frightened and gave him everything she had in the house (for this ogre was not a bad husband, even though he did eat little children). Once he was loaded up with all the ogre's treasure, therefore, Little Thummie returned with it to his father's house, where he was received with great joy.

However, there are plenty of people who dispute the truth of this last circumstance, and who claim that Little Thummie never robbed the ogre in this way, although it is true that he did not scruple to take his seven league boots, because they were only used for running after little children.

These people maintain (saying that they have it on the best authority having actually eaten and drunk in the woodcutter's house), that when Little Thummie had put on the ogre's boots, he took himself off to the Court, where he knew there to be great anxiety over the fate of the Army, which was two hundred leagues away, and the outcome of a battle in which it had been engaged. They say he sought out the King, and told him that if he wished, he would bring him news of his troops before the end of the day. The King promised him a huge reward if he succeeded, and Little Thummie delivered his report that same evening. Having made his name by this first errand, he was able to obtain everything he wanted, for the King paid him handsomely for carrying his orders to the Army, and countless ladies gave him anything he asked in order to have news of their lovers— and this was where he made his greatest profit.

(There were also some wives who charged him with letters for their husbands, but they paid him so poorly, and it amounted to so little, that he did not bother to keep account of what he earned from that source.)

After having followed this career as a courier for some

time, and having amassed a considerable fortune by it, he returned to his father's house.

It is impossible to imagine the joy with which he was welcomed. He was able to make his whole family comfortable, by buying important positions for his father and brothers—thereby establishing them all in prosperity and providing the King with faithful servants at the same time.

Dear Madame,

I am glad that my tale of Thummie suited the occasion, but sorry that Mademoiselle's tender heart was so afflicted by the fate of the little ogresses. She seems to feel that my hero's glory must be tarnished more than somewhat by responsibility for their deaths. But only think—it could not have happened, had not their father been bent on murder!

However, I am entirely content to bow to her complaints on another score. She is quite right. In my disquisition on fairytales I did indeed commend several as particularly distinguished examples of their kind, yet so far I have not sent you a single one of them. But I have my defence already prepared. It is that I have been giving more than usual care to their presentation, and now that the first is ready for your perusal, I hope you will think the result worth my pains.

You are right, Madame, in your recollection of 'Griselidis' as a little book in blue paper covers, bought from a pedlar's pack, but it is of nobler descent than that, and I have tried to do it justice.

My dear Mademoiselle, you who are young, beautiful and wise, as I offer you this model of Patience, I do not by any means delude myself that you will follow it in every detail; that would be too much in all conscience. But here in Paris, where men are so smooth-spoken, and where the fair sex, born to please, finds this destiny so happily fulfilled, so many examples of fickle pride are to be seen on all sides, that it is impossible to have too much of the antidote for one's protection.

A lady as constant as the one whose worth is demonstrated in this story, would be a thing of wonder anywhere, but in Paris she would be a prodigy. The ladies here wield sovereign power: everything is ordered according to their wishes, in short it is a happy clime, in which every woman is a queen. So I can see that Griselidis will be little valued here. Rather she will provide a subject for laughter, with her old-fashioned lessons.

It is not that the ladies of Paris do not regard patience as a virtue, but by long practice they have acquired the art of making their husbands exercise it . . .

Griselidis

AT the foot of those famous mountains, where the Po emerges from its reeds to take its new-born waters wandering into the heart of the neighbouring lands, there lived a young and valiant Prince, the pride of his people. When forming him Heaven had poured out all its rarest gifts with such extravagant generosity as it shows only to great kings. Richly endowed with every excellence of mind and body, he stood head and shoulders above his friends and contemporaries.

He was strong, athletic and well suited to the craft of War, yet prompted by a secret spark of genius he was also ardently devoted to the Arts of Peace. He delighted in battles and Victory, grand strategies, courageous acts and all that immortalises a fair reputation in History, but his sympathetic and generous heart was still more aware of the lasting glory of making his people happy.

However, this heroic character was clouded by a gloomy cast of mind, a miasma of unfounded cynicism and melancholy, which made him believe at the bottom of his heart, that all the fair sex were faithless and deceitful. Even in a woman who shone with the rarest excellence, he saw a hypocritical soul, a mind drunk with pride, a cruel despot, whose one unrelenting aspiration was to gain absolute power over any unhappy man who was delivered into her hands. The common custom of the world, whereby all husbands seem to be either down-trodden or betrayed, along with the jealous temperament of his race, further increased this deep hatred for women. More than once, therefore, he swore that even if Heaven in its generosity should frame for him another Lucrece, he would never submit to the bonds of matrimony.

His bachelor life was ordered by a daily routine which never varied. In the morning, which he gave up to business, he dealt wisely with all matters pertaining to the just governing of his realm. He might be concerned, for instance, with protecting the rights of defenceless orphans and oppressed widows, or with removing some tax, which an unavoidable war had forced him to impose earlier. The other half of the day he dedicated to the hunt, pursuing wild boars and bears, which for all their ferocity and strength, yet alarmed him less than the charming sex, which he avoided rigorously.

Meanwhile, knowing that their best interests demanded that they be sure of a successor to their Prince, who would govern them with the same consideration as he had, his subjects urged him ceaselessly to give them an heir, eventually coming all together in a body to the palace to make one last effort.

An orator with an impressively dignified bearing, the most eloquent man of his time, said all that could be said in such circumstances. He placed on record their pressing desire to see a fortunate posterity proceed from the Prince, expatiated at length on how this would ensure that their state would flourish forever, and told him in conclusion, that he saw a new-born star rising, issue of his chaste nuptials, beside which the moon itself looked pale.

In a manner more simple and a voice less powerful and ringing, the Prince replied to his subjects in this fashion:

'The warmth and enthusiasm with which you urge me to accept the bonds of matrimony, are pleasing to me, as welcome evidence of your love. I am deeply moved, and wish that I could satisfy your wishes at the earliest possible date, but to my mind marriage is a business in which the more prudent a man is, the longer he delays.

'Take a close look at the way young girls behave: as long as they live in the bosom of their families, they are all virtue, prudence, modesty and sincerity, but marriage quickly puts an end to the disguise. Once their future is settled, it no longer matters about being well-behaved; they abandon the role, which they took such pains to keep up before, and each conducts herself in her own household according to her fancy. One, having a peevish disposition, incapable of being amused, becomes exaggeratedly devout, always crying out on the world and disapproving of everything; another turns into a coquette, gossips endlessly and can never have enough lovers. This young woman becomes passionately interested in the Arts, pronounces arrogantly on everything, criticises even the most talented authors, and in a word, assumes all the affectations of a Précieuse. This other sets herself up as a gambler, losing everything – money, jewels, rings, valuable furniture, and even her very clothes.

'In all the diversity of the roads they take, I see only one thing they have in common – they all want to lay down the law. Now, I am convinced that in matrimony it is impossible to live happily, when both parties are giving orders. If, therefore, you want me to commit myself to marriage, find a young beauty without pride or vanity, totally obedient, whose patience is tested and proven, and who has not the least trace of self-will. When you have found her, I will marry her.'

Having made an end of this moral discourse, the Prince leaps on his horse and races away at a breathless pace to join his pack of hounds, which await him in open country. He gallops over meadows and ploughed fields, to find his hunters lying on the green grass. They jump up all alert, and make the multitude of forest creatures tremble with the sound of their horns. The noisy canine tribe runs here and there among the shining stubble, and the bloodhounds with fiery eyes, used for hunting beasts out of their lairs, drag after them as they search, the sturdy servants, who hold them leashed.

Being informed by one of his men, that all is ready, and the scent has been picked up, he orders that the hunt begin immediately, and has the hounds released after the stag. The note of the resounding horns, the neighing of horses and the penetrating bay of the excited hounds, fill the forest with uproar and confusion which, endlessly redoubled by echoes, carry into the deepest hollows of the woods.

On this occasion, however, by chance or Destiny, it happened that the Prince took a path which diverged from the one followed by the rest of the hunt. The further he went, the further he became separated from his people, until at last he had gone so far astray, that he could no longer hear the sound of dogs and horns.

The place of clear streams and sombre foliage to which his strange adventure led him, possessed his spirits with a profound awe. The innocence and simplicity of Nature seemed so beautiful and so pure, that he blessed a thousand times the mistake which had brought him there. Lost as he was in pleasant reveries, inspired by the great trees, the streams and glades, he was suddenly confronted by the most attractive sight, the most gentle and lovable, that he had ever seen under heaven. He was stricken to the heart.

A young shepherdess sat spinning on the bank of a stream, twisting her nimble spindle with a skilful and housewifely hand, while she watched over her flock. A glimpse of her would have tamed the most savage heart; her complexion was as fair as the lily and its natural freshness had always been protected by the shade of the groves, in which she lived. Her mouth had all the charm of childhood, and her eyes, shaded by a dusky eyelid, were more blue than the sky and more luminous.

The Prince crept enraptured through the wood to gaze on the beauty, which had moved his soul, but the lovely girl heard his stealthy movements and turned towards him. From the moment she knew that she was observed, the swift and lively warmth of a vivid blush redoubled the splendour of her fair complexion, and modesty triumphed in her shining countenance.

Under the innocent veil of this graceful shame, the Prince discerned a simplicity, a gentleness, a sincerity of which he had believed the fair sex to be incapable, but which he saw there in all their beauty.

Seized by a fear quite new to him, disconcerted and more timid even than she, he approached and told her in a trembling voice, that he had lost track of all his huntsmen, and asked her if the hunt had passed through any part of that wood.

'My Lord, I have seen nothing in this lonely place,' she said. 'And no one else has been here but you alone. But don't worry. I can direct you back to a path you will know.'

'I cannot thank the Gods too much for my happy fate,' said the Prince. 'For a long time I have frequented this forest, but I knew nothing until today of the most precious thing it contains.'

As he spoke, he knelt down on the moist bank of the

stream to quench his burning thirst from its waters. Seeing this she said:

'My Lord, wait a moment!'

And running quickly to her hut, she fetched a cup, which she happily and willingly presented to her new admirer. Precious vessels of crystal and agate, glittering in a thousand places with gold and fashioned with care by delicate artistry, had never seemed to him so beautiful in their useless ostentation as the pottery bowl, which the shepherdess gave him.

To find a good road which would take the Prince back to the town, they had to go through the heart of the forest, passing sheer crags and broken torrents. Their path wound this way and that, but the Prince did not turn into any new track, without taking careful note of all the local landmarks, for his sharp-witted love, which already intended to return, was making a faithful map of the route. At last the shepherdess led him to the cool shade of a grove, where from beneath the tangled branches he could see in the distance, in the middle of the plain, the golden roofs of his great palace. As he took leave of his lovely guide, he was touched by a sharp pain, and moved away from her with slow steps, burdened by the dart which had pierced his heart. The memory of his delightful adventure accompanied him pleasantly to his home, but next morning he began to feel the pain of his wound, and seemed overwhelmed by sorrow and anxiety.

As soon as he could he returned to the hunt, and cunningly evading his entourage, he escaped to lose himself happily in the forest once again. The high tops of hills and trees, which he had so carefully observed, along with the secret guidance of his faithful love, directed him so well, that in spite of a hundred different roads crossing his, he found the dwelling of his young shepherdess. He learned that her name was Griselidis, that she had no family in the world but her father, that they lived peacefully on the milk of their

ewes, and that they made their clothes, without recourse to
the town, from their own fleeces, which she alone spun.

The more he saw of her, the more fiercely the fire of love
burned in him, kindled by the glowing perfections of her
soul. He learned through closer acquaintance with these
gifts, that the shepherdess's beauty was only an outward
manifestation of the animating spirit which shone in her eyes.
Ever and again he was overwhelmed with joy at having
bestowed his first love so well, and so, without more delay,
he assembled his council, and made this speech to them:

'At last in accordance with your wishes I am going to
marry. I do not intend to take my wife – beautiful, virtuous
and well-born – from some foreign land, but from among
you, as my ancestors have done more than once. However, I
am not going to inform you of my choice until the great day
itself.'

The moment the news was released, it spread like
wildfire. The warmth with which the people expressed their
gladness throughout the city was indescribable. Happiest of
all was the orator, who believed himself to be the sole author
of this great event, by means of his moving speech. What an
important man he thought himself! Nothing can resist great
eloquence, he told himself repeatedly in his heart.

It was a pleasure to see the futile efforts all the society
beauties made to attract their Lord the Prince, hoping to be
worthy of his choice. Knowing he was charmed more by a
chaste and modest air than by anything else, just as he had
said a hundred times, they all changed their clothing and
bearing completely. They softened their voices – even
coughed in a devout tone – lowered their hairstyles by half a
foot, covered their bosoms, lengthened their sleeves and one
could hardly see the little tips of their toes, under their skirts.

As the day of the wedding approaches, every art can be
seen diligently at work in the town. Here magnificent
carriages are being made in quite a new style, so handsome
and so cleverly devised, that the gold which glitters on them

everywhere forms the least of their attractions. There long platforms are erected, so that the spectators can see all the pomp of the pageantry easily and without obstruction. Here great triumphal arches rise, on which the warrior Prince's glory is celebrated, and Love's dazzling victory over him. There, with cunning skill, those fires are wrought, which frightening the earth with claps of innocent thunder, embellish the skies with a thousand new stars. Here the pleasant folly of an ingenious ballet is painstakingly devised, and there one hears being rehearsed the melodious airs of an opera, with a cast of a thousand gods, the finest thing that ever came out of Italy.

At last the great day of the Wedding, the long-awaited, much-talked-of Wedding, arrived.

The rosy dawn had hardly mingled gold with blue on the background of a bright, pure sky, when all the fair sex throughout the land awoke with a start. Full of curiosity the people surrounded the Palace on all sides, so that guards had to be posted at various points to contain the crowds and keep them in their places. The whole building resounded with bugles, flutes, oboes and rustic bagpipes, while nothing could be heard in the area around it but trumpets and drums.

Eventually the Prince came out, surrounded by his Court. A great shout of joy went up, but what was everyone's surprise, when at the first crossroads he took the road towards the nearby forest, just as he did every day. 'There you are!' they all cried in amazement. 'That's his real passion. Hunting still has the strongest hold over him, in spite of Love!'

Swiftly he crossed the ploughlands of the plain, and reaching the mountains, to the great astonishment of the accompanying troop of courtiers, he entered the forest. Following winding paths, which his enamoured heart rejoiced to recognise, he found at last the rural lodging, which sheltered his tenderest hopes.

At that very moment Griselidis, dressed in her best

clothes, was coming out of her rustic cottage, for she had heard rumours of the Wedding and was going to see the magnificent ceremonial herself.

The Prince approached her.

'Where are you running to, so swift and lightfooted?' he said, gazing at her tenderly. 'There's no need for you to hurry, sweet shepherdess: the wedding to which you are going, and in which I am the bridegroom, cannot go ahead without you. It is you that I love, you that I have chosen from a thousand beautiful girls, you with whom I would spend the rest of my life, if only my declaration of love is not rejected.'

'Ah, my Lord!' she said. 'I cannot believe that I am destined for this supreme glory: you are only seeking to amuse yourself at my expense.'

'No, no,' he said. 'I mean it. Your father is already on my side.' (The Prince had taken care to warn him of what he intended.) 'All that remains is for you to deign to consent. But so that there may be a secure tranquillity between us forever, you must swear never to have any will but mine.'

'I swear it,' she said. 'And I can assure you, that if I had married the meanest man in the village, I should have obeyed him, and the yoke of his authority would have seemed light to me. How much more, then, if you are to be both my Lord and my husband.'

In this way, therefore, the Prince made public his intention, and while the Court applauded his choice, he prevailed upon Griselidis to allow herself to be arrayed in the manner befitting a King's bride. Those ladies whose duties involved them in this task, entered the cottage, where they busied themselves with putting all their experience and skill into arranging every detail of her costume with grace. As they crowded into the tiny house, the ladies were full of admiration for the ingenuity with which poverty was concealed by good housekeeping, and this rustic bothy, sheltered and shaded by a spreading plane tree, seemed to them an enchanted place.

At last the charming shepherdess emerged, stately and brilliant, from her retreat. There was nothing but praise for her beauty and her clothes, but under all this unfamiliar formality, the Prince already regretted more than once the innocent simplicity of her peasant dress.

Full of majesty, she took her place on a great chariot of gold and ivory. The prince mounted proudly at her side, and did not think it less glorious to be seen beside her as a lover, than to march in a triumphal procession after some victory. The Court came after them, all in order according to their office or the nobility of their blood.

The whole town had turned out into the fields, covering the countryside round about, and having been told of the Prince's choice, awaited his return with impatience. The moment he appeared, the people pressed up to him. The chariot could hardly move through the dense crowd, which parted slowly ahead of it. Disturbed and excited by the prolonged cheering, which was constantly renewed, the horses reared, danced and plunged, often moving backwards more than they advanced.

At last the couple arrived at the church, where by the eternal chain of a solemn promise, they united their destinies.

After this they returned to the palace, where a thousand entertainments awaited them. Dances, games, races and tourneys filled the rest of the day. And the night was crowned by the chaste tenderness of the lovely bride.

The following day the provincial assemblies all over the country hastened to send their magistrates to convey their greetings to the Prince and Princess.

Surrounded by her ladies, and without appearing the least bit disconcerted, Griselidis listened to them like a Princess and like a Princess she replied. She did everything with so much discretion, that it seemed as if Heaven had endowed her mind with its treasures even more abundantly than her body. Her intelligence aided by her keen insight at once grasped the manners of the great world. Even from the

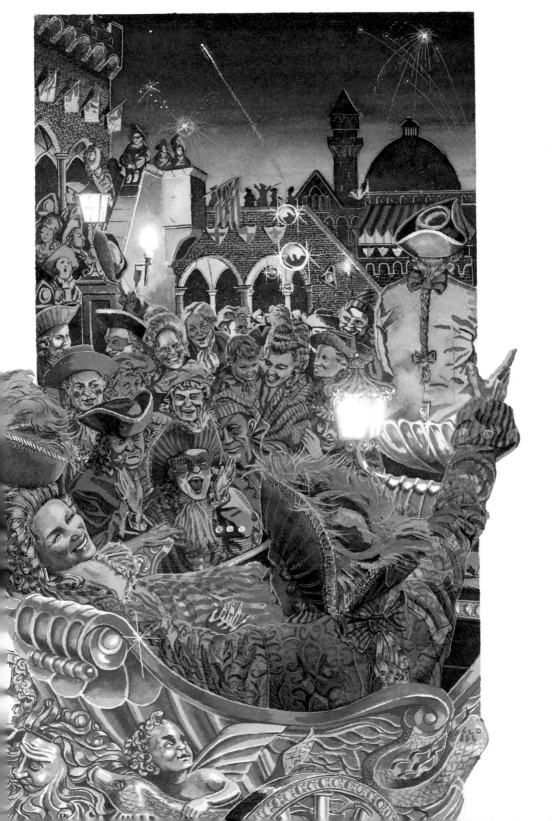

first day she was so well informed about the characters and accomplishments of the ladies of her Court, that her sound judgement, which nothing ever discomposed, had less trouble managing them than she had experienced with her ewes in the old days.

Before the end of the year, Heaven blessed their fortune-favoured bed with the fruits of marriage. It was not the much wished-for Prince, but a young Princess, so beautiful, that no one could have wished her not to have been born. She seemed so exquisite and charming to her father, that he came to look at her every other moment, while her mother, still more enchanted, gazed on her unceasingly.

She wanted to nurse the child herself.

'How can I excuse myself from the duty, which her cries demand of me, without the worst sort of ingratitude?' she said. 'Can I be willing to be only half a mother to the child I love? It would do violence to Nature.'

However, as the heat of the Prince's ardour decreased from the intensity of its earliest days, so the smouldering mass of his evil melancholy flared up again. Its thick fumes obscured his sense and corrupted his heart. He imagined nothing the Princess did to be sincere; her virtue itself offended him – it was too great, it must be a trap for his credulity. His uneasy mind was disturbed and confused, believed every suspicion, and took pleasure in casting doubt on the excess of his happiness.

Seeking to cure the disease with which his soul was infected, he followed her, watched her, took pleasure in distressing her with tiresome constraints, sudden shocks or anything he thought might disentangle truth from sham.

'It will not let me sleep,' he said. 'If her virtues are genuine, the most insufferable treatment will only confirm them.'

He kept her shut up in her palace, far from all the amusements of the Court, and hardly allowed the light of day to enter the room where she lived in solitary retirement.

Claiming that the fairest adornment for a woman was the glorious regalia of femininity, formed by Nature itself to delight the eye, he demanded in unmannerly fashion, that she return the pearls, rubies, rings and jewellery, which he had given her as a mark of tenderness, when he became her husband.

She whose life was without blemish, and who had never had any ambition but to do her duty, gave them to him without the least concern. Indeed seeing that he was pleased to take them back, she actually felt no less joy in returning them, than she had in receiving them.

'My husband torments me in order to test me,' she said to herself. 'It's quite clear that he only makes me suffer in order to reawaken my listless virtue, which could fade away through too long and sweet a rest. Even if that is not his intention at least I am sure that it is God's will for me, and that the tedious duration of so many hardships, is only meant to train my faith and constancy. So many unhappy souls, led by their own desires, stray down a thousand dangerous roads after false and empty pleasures, while the Lord in his slow justice allows them to go to the edge of the abyss without intervening to save them. But by a pure impulse of His supreme goodness, he has chosen me, like a child he loves, and has set Himself to correct me. I should therefore love the cruel severity he employs to teach me. We can only be happy in the same measure as we suffer: we should love His fatherly goodness, and the hand of which it makes use.'

The Prince saw her obey all his tyrannical orders without reservation, but still was not convinced.

'I can see how she maintains this pretended virtue,' he said. 'And what it is that renders all my assaults on it ineffective. It is because they only touch her in things to which she is now indifferent. All her tenderness is given to her child, to the young Princess: I should be paying more attention to that, for there, if anywhere, I can clarify the matter.'

When he went to his wife, she had just fed the child she loved so intensely. The baby lay against her breast and played with her, laughing as she looked up at her.

'I can see how much you love her,' he said. 'Nevertheless even at this tender age I have to take her away from you, to begin her education, and to preserve her from certain bad habits she might catch from you. I have been fortunate enough to find a lady of intelligence, who will be able to bring her up with all the accomplishments and polished manners a princess ought to have. Be ready to part with her – someone will come to take her away.'

At that he left her, having neither the courage nor the inhumanity to see the sole pledge of their love torn from her. Her face bathed with tears, she waited in deep dejection for the dreadful moment when this calamity should overtake her.

But as soon as the hated man appeared, who was to carry out this sad, cruel order, she said:

'I must obey.'

She took the child she loved so dearly, whose little arms hugged her tenderly, and kissed her with all the intensity of a mother, then dissolving in tears, she gave her up. What bitter pain that was! To tear her child from the breast of so tender a mother, must be as agonising as to tear out her heart.

Near the city there was a convent, famous and long established, where the nuns lived by an austere rule under the eyes of an Abbess distinguished for her piety. There in the silence of the cloister the child was left, without her birth being revealed, though some valuable jewels were left also, as a guarantee of future payment in keeping with the care that would be taken of her.

The Prince turned to hunting again, trying to shed the burden of remorse for his monstrous cruelty. He was also as much afraid to face the Princess, as he might have been to meet a proud tigress, whose cub he had just taken from her. However, she continued to treat him not merely with gentleness, but with every mark of affection, even with the same tenderness she had shown to him in the happier days of her glory.

Her willingness to comply, so great and so prompt, touched him with shame and regret. But his black emotions were unchanged, if anything growing still darker. Two days later, therefore, feigning tears in order to injure her the more deeply, he came to tell her that their beloved child was dead.

This unexpected blow wounded her to the heart. Nevertheless, in spite of her grief, when she saw how pale her husband was, she seemed to forget her own misfortune and to feel nothing but a tender anxiety to console his pretended pain.

Such goodness, such an unequalled warmth of wifely love, all at once disarmed the Prince's hostility. He was touched keenly; his feelings were transformed, even to the point of wishing he could tell her that their child was still alive. But the evil mood raised its head again and proudly forbade him to reveal anything of his secret: it might be useful to keep quiet about it.

From that happy day onwards, such was the mutual love of husband and wife, that the tenderness of Lover and Mistress in their sweetest moments could not have been greater. Fifteen times the Sun, ordering the seasons, dwelt turn by turn in each of his twelve houses, without seeing any division between them. If the Prince sometimes took a capricious pleasure in upsetting his wife, it was only to prevent love from fading, just as the blacksmith, hurrying on his work, sometimes spills a little water on the embers of his listless forge to increase its heat.

Meanwhile the young Princess grew in intelligence and goodness. To the gentleness and simplicity, which she had inherited from her sweet mother, was added her illustrious father's proud nobility. The combination of all that was most pleasing in each character added up to a perfect beauty. She shone like a star, wherever she went, and by chance she was seen at the convent grille by a young lord of the Court, an extremely handsome young man, who fell passionately in love with her. Through that natural feminine instinct possessed by all beautiful women, of seeing the invisible wound their eyes inflict at the very moment the deed is done, the Princess was aware of his love. After resisting it for some time, as was only proper before yielding, she on her side came to love him with an equal tenderness.

There was nothing in this love to provoke disapprobation. The young man was handsome, valiant and descended from distinguished ancestors. In fact the Prince had been casting an eye in his direction for some time, with the idea of making him his son-in-law. He was therefore delighted to learn of the mutual love with which this young couple burned. But he was possessed by a peculiar desire to make them buy the greatest happiness of their life with cruel suffering.

'I shall be glad to make them happy,' he said. 'But their love must be deepened and confirmed by facing the harsh storms of anguish. At the same time I will put my wife's patience to the test. Not as formerly to reassure my insane mistrust – I can no longer doubt her love – but to display her goodness, her gentleness, her profound wisdom before the eyes of all the world, so that the Earth, seeing itself adorned with these great and precious gifts, may be filled with reverence, and in recognition give thanks for them to Heaven.'

Accordingly he made a public announcement, in which he pointed out that, since the daughter of his foolish marriage had died almost as soon as she was born, he had no family from which the state might one day find another lord. Therefore he must now look elsewhere for better fortune. He added that the wife he meant to take was of noble birth, and that she had been raised until then in a convent in complete innocence of the world.

You may judge what cruel news this was to the young

lovers, when the Princess learned that she was to be the Prince's bride.

Next, without any show of either anger or sorrow, he told his faithful wife that he must part from her in order to avert a terrible misfortune. He explained that the people, indignant over her low birth, were forcing him to make a worthier match elsewhere.

'You will have to return to your roof of thatch and bracken,' he said. 'And resume your shepherdess's dress, which I have had prepared for you.'

With calm, mute constancy the Princess heard her sentence pronounced. Behind a mask of serenity she swallowed her pain. Great tears fell from her lovely eyes, without lessening her beauty, just as sunshine and rain sometimes mingle in early Spring.

She sighed, almost on the point of fainting.

'You are my husband, my lord and my master,' she said. 'And however frightful your words, I will show you, that nothing is so dear to me as to obey you.'

At once she withdrew alone to her chamber, where she stripped herself of her rich garments. Peaceably and without a word, although she sighed in her heart, she resumed those she had worn when she minded her ewes.

In this plain and humble dress she approached the Prince.

'I cannot leave you without begging your pardon for having displeased you,' she said. 'I can endure the weight of my wretchedness, my Lord, but I cannot endure your anger. If you only have mercy on my sincere penitence, I shall live content in my sad exile, and Time will never change either my humble respect or my faithful love.'

Such submission and such greatness of soul so meanly clad, at once reawakened in the Prince's heart every detail of his first love, and he was on the point of revoking the decree of her banishment. Moved by her compelling charm, and ready to weep, he took a step towards her, meaning to take her in his arms. But then his overbearing pride in holding firm to his purpose, triumphed over his love, and he replied severely:

'All that is past has gone from my memory. I am glad of your repentance. Go, it is time to leave.'

She departed immediately with her father, who was also dressed once again in his peasant clothes.

'Come,' she said to the old man, who was bitter, bewildered and distressed by such a swift and sudden change. 'Let us go back to our dark woodlands, back to our home in the wilds of the country. We've no reason to regret the pomp and ceremony of palaces – our cottage is not so magnificent, but more innocence is to be found there, as well as a more secure repose and a sweeter peace.'

It was a hard and painful journey, but she came at last to her wilderness, where she took up again her distaff and her spindle, and went to spin beside the same stream, where the Prince had first seen her. Her tranquil heart, free of all bitterness, prayed Heaven a hundred times a day to heap her husband with glory and riches, and refuse none of his desires. A love nourished with kindness could not have been more devoted than hers.

After a while this dear husband for whom she sorrowed, still wishing even now to test her, sent word to her in her retreat, that she should come to him.

'Griselidis,' he said, as soon as she presented herself. 'Tomorrow in church I am to give my hand to a young Princess, and you and I must make her happy. I want you to help me please her, and I am asking you to put all your efforts into this. You know how I must be served, without stint or reservation. Employ all your skill in preparing her apartments, so that luxury, splendour, seemliness and elegance are all equally apparent there. And never forget that this is a Princess whom I love dearly.

'So that you will enter more fully into the responsibilities of your duty, I want to show you the lady whom I have ordered you to serve.'

When the Princess entered, she appeared like the new Dawn showing herself at the gates of the eastern skies, but yet more beautiful. Griselidis felt a shock of maternal tenderness in the depths of her heart. The memory of times past, of her days of happiness and good fortune, returned to her.

'If Heaven had heard my prayers favourably,' she said to herself, 'my own daughter would have been as old as this, and perhaps as beautiful.'

In that moment she conceived a love so warm and strong for the young Princess, that as soon as the girl was gone, she spoke freely to the Prince, following her natural instinct without realising it.

'My Lord,' she said. 'Permit me to remind you that this delightful Princess, whose husband you are about to become, has been reared as a great lady, in comfort and luxury. She will not be able to stand the treatment I have received from you without endangering her life. Need and obscure birth had hardened me to bearing burdens, and I could endure all sorts of troubles without difficulty, and even without complaint. But she has never known distress: she will die at the first word that sounds a little curt, or a little harsh. My Lord, I beg you to treat her with gentleness!'

'Content yourself with serving me according to your ability,' said the Prince in a severe tone. 'There's no need for a simple shepherdess to set herself up as a teacher and start lecturing me on my duty.'

At these words Griselidis lowered her eyes and withdrew without saying anything.

Meanwhile the nobility invited to the wedding were arriving from all directions. The Prince gathered them together in a magnificent hall before the ceremony began, and spoke to them in this fashion:

'Nothing in the world, Hope excepted, is more deceptive than Appearances, and here you may see a glaring example of this. Who would not believe that my young mistress, whom marriage is about to make into a Princess, must be happy and light of heart?

'They would be wrong.

'Who could avoid supposing that this young warrior, in love with honour, must be glad of this wedding, which gives him the opportunity to triumph over all his rivals in the tourneys to be held.

'All the same, it is not true.

'Who would believe, moreover, that Griselidis is not weeping and despairing in justified anger?

'Yet she makes not the least complaint: she accepts everything, and nothing has been able to tire her patience.

'Finally, who, seeing the beauty of my bride, would not think the happiness of my destiny beyond comparison?

'Nevertheless, if I bind myself in this marriage, I should find in it nothing but profound grief, and of all the Princes in the world, I should be the most unfortunate.

'This riddle seems inpenetrable to you; two words will make all plain, and those two words will cause all the misfortunes you have just heard to vanish.

'Know then,' he continued, 'that the lovely creature, whom you believe to have wounded my heart, is in fact my daughter, and that I am giving her in marriage to this young lord, who loves her passionately, and whom she loves as much in return.

'You should further know, that touched to the heart by the patience and devotion of the faithful, virtuous wife I have hounded without cause, I am taking her back, so that I may compensate her with all that is kindest in love, for the hard and barbarous treatment she has received from my jealous spirit. I shall be more eager in future to anticipate her every wish, than I was in my confusion of mind to heap distresses upon her. And if the afflictions which never subdued her heart, must live in men's memories for all time, I hope they will speak yet more of the glory with which I shall crown her supreme virtue.'

Sometimes, when the day is darkened by heavy clouds, and the lowering sky threatens a fearful storm, this gloomy veil may be parted by the wind, allowing a brilliant ray of sunlight to spill across the landscape, and the whole world laughs and recovers its beauty. Even so in all the eyes where sadness had reigned, an intense happiness now shone.

The young Princess, overjoyed to learn by this sudden enlightenment, that the Prince was her father, threw herself at his feet and embraced his knees. Her father lifted her up, kissed her and led her to her mother, who was almost reft of her senses by too much happiness all at once. Her heart which had borne grief so well, though so often ravaged by the fierce darts of misfortune, now sank under the gentle burden of joy. She was barely able to clasp the beloved child, restored to her by heaven. She could only weep.

'You will have many other opportunities to satisfy your love for your child,' the Prince told her. 'You must now change back into the clothes befitting your rank—we have a marriage to make.'

The two young lovers were conveyed to church, where they affirmed their fond attachment for all time by the promise to cherish each other with loving-kindness.

Then there was nothing but entertainments, magnificent tourneys, music, dancing and lavish banquets, at which all eyes were turned towards Griselidis, and her long-tried patience was exalted to Heaven in a thousand eulogies. The rejoicing people were so happy for their capricious Prince, that they almost went so far as to commend his cruel testing, since it had produced such a perfect model of such exquisite virtue, so becoming to the fair sex, and so rare in any place.

Dear Madame,

After your praise of 'Griselidis', you said that you hesitated to offer your few criticisms. I assure you, no one else has been so reticent. Indeed, had I followed all the different advice, which has been given to me on this work in the last week or so, nothing would remain but the bare story alone, in which case I had done better not to have touched it at all, but to have left it in its blue paper covers, as it has been for so many years.

Shall I tell you all about it?

First I read it to two friends of ours.

'Why go on so much about your hero's style of living?' said one. 'What does it matter what he does in his council in the morning, still less how he amuses himself in the afternoon? That ought to come out.'

'I implore you,' said the other, 'to remove the jocular response the Prince makes to the deputies of his people, when they urge him to marry; it isn't at all what one would expect of a serious, dignified ruler. Then there's that long description of the hunt,' he continued. 'How does that matter to the essence of your story? Take my word for it, these are empty, ostentatious decorations, which impoverish your poem instead of enriching it. The same goes for the preparations for the Prince's marriage—it's all trifling and pointless. As for your ladies lowering their hairstyles, covering their bosoms

and lengthening their sleeves—' he added, 'all mere
mechanical foolery, like the bit about the orator applauding
his own eloquence.'

'I wish you would also cut out Griselidis's meditations,
when she says it must be God, who is testing her,' said the one
who had spoken first. 'That's a piece of quite inappropriate
sermonising. And I don't know how to bear your Prince's
inhumanity!' (I think you would agree with that, Madame?)
'It puts me in such a rage—personally I'd suppress that part.
It's true that it's in the original story, but I don't see that it
matters. I'd also leave out the young lord, who's only there to
marry the young princess—that episode makes your narrative
far too long.'

'But the story has a very poor ending without him,' I said.

'Well, I don't know about that,' he replied. 'I know I
wouldn't hesitate to cut him myself.'

Several days later I did the same reading to two other
friends, who said not a word about the parts I've just
detailed, but reproved plenty of others!

When they had done, they feared they might have
offended me.

'Not at all,' I said. 'Far be it from me to complain of the
severity of your criticism. I might rather complain that it isn't
severe enough, for you've let me off on an endless number of
points, which have been found worthy of censure.'

'Such as?' they asked.

'I have been told that I make too much of the Prince's
character,' I said. 'And that there is no need to know what he
did in the morning, and still less in the afternoon.'

'Someone's making fun of you,' they said, both together, 'if
they offer criticisms like that.'

'The reply the Prince makes to those who urge him to
marry, has been condemned as too jocular and unworthy of a
serious and dignified ruler,' I continued.

'Fine,' one of them replied. 'What's so unsuitable about a
young Italian prince being a little humorous on the subject of

matrimony? After all, in that country it's quite customary to see the most dignified and exalted of men joking in public. Some of them almost make a profession of slandering both women and marriage, which you must admit are common enough topics of raillery. At all events, I ask your mercy on that part, and for the orator who hopes to convert the Prince, and the lowering of the hair-dos—for someone who didn't like the Prince's jokes, would be just the sort to take a strong line on those too.'

'You've guessed right,' I said. 'But on the other hand, those who only enjoy cheerful things, can't endure the Princess's Christian meditation, in which she supposes that God wishes to test her. They claim that this is inappropriate sermonising.'

'Inappropriate?' replied the other. 'I would have said that these religious reflections are not only in keeping with the Princess's character, but are absolutely necessary to the story! You've got to make your heroine's patience credible, and what other means have you, than to make her regard her husband's mistreatment as proceeding from the hand of God? Without that she might be taken for the stupidest of women, rather than the most virtuous, which surely would not be the impression you would wish to create?'

'Fault has also been found with the episode of the young lord, who marries the young princess,' I said.

'They've got it all wrong,' my friend replied. 'Although you call your work a novella, it is in fact a poem, so there must be nothing untidy or unpleasing about the ending. If the young princess were to be sent back to her convent without being married, after expecting to be, neither she nor your readers would be best pleased.'

After this conference I made up my mind to allow my work to be read in the Academy much as it stands. In short, I took some pains to correct things, which had been shown to be bad in themselves, but those parts that had no other fault, than that they were not to the taste of my more finicky acquaintances, I reckoned I could leave alone.

Do you send a good dish back to the kitchen, just because there is a guest at your table who happens not to like it, Madame? Of course not. We must live and let live, and if everyone is to be kept happy, the dishes on the table must be as varied as the tastes of the diners.

So what do you think I should do about publishing this piece?

I think I ought to take the first opportunity to put my work before the public, which is always the best judge. Then I shall learn from my readers what I really ought to do, and if ever I issue a second edition, I shall exactly follow all their opinions.

But you and Mademoiselle have had enough of Griselidis. You are already demanding the next, and my little friend insists that it shall be a happy story. Nothing could suit me better.

I know that some of my acquaintance have such serious minds, behind brows ever furrowed with thought, that they can never approve of any but the most formal and exalted literary tone. But, as you are aware, I believe that there are times when even the highest intellect may enjoy a puppet show without blushing, and occasions when pleasant trifles are more valuable to us than solemn and serious reflections. I see nothing surprising in the fact that even the most judicious reason sometimes tires of wakefulness, and is content to be rocked into a pleasant doze by tales of ogres and fays.

So, I have no serious fear that you will condemn me for employing my leisure wastefully, if I comply with your entirely reasonable request, that I relate at length the tale of Donkeyskin . . .

Donkeyskin

THERE was once a King, the greatest that ever lived: kindly in Peace, terrible in War – in short, none could compare with him. His neighbours feared him, his people were tranquil, and everywhere under the protection of his power both Art and Virtue flourished freely. His lovely wife, the faithful companion of a lifetime, was so charming and beautiful, with such a gentle and accommodating spirit, that he was even more fortunate as a husband than he was as a king. Their happy and devoted marriage, so rich in tenderness and satisfaction, had produced only one child, a daughter who had so many excellent qualities, that they were easily consoled for having no larger family.

In the King's vast and opulent palace there was nothing that was not magnificent. A busy host of courtiers and servants swarmed everywhere, and his stables were full of every kind of horse, large and small, all covered with fine caparisons, stiff with gold and embroidery. But what surprised everyone who entered these stables, was that in the place of honour stood a fine, big ass wagging his two long ears.

This strange distinction given to such a vulgar creature may surprise you, but when you are acquainted with the animal's incomparable virtues, you will no longer think the honour paid it too great. It had been so wonderfully formed by Nature, that it never produced dung, but all manner of beautiful shining gold coins, which were collected up first thing every morning from the golden straw.

Now Heaven, which sometimes tires of making men happy, and which always mingles some hardship with its blessings, like showers and fine weather, suddenly allowed a cruel sickness to ravage the Queen's fair days. Help was sought everywhere, but neither the doctors of the Faculty, who studied Hippocrates and Galen, nor the fashionable quacks, were able with all their combined efforts to arrest the fever, which burned ever more fiercely.

Being come to her last hour, she said to the King her husband:

'I wish that before I die, you might see fit to let me ask one thing of you: that if you want to marry again when I am no more . . .'

'Ah, this is all quite unnecessary!' said the King. 'I could never in my life think of it; be easy on that count.'

'I must believe you,' replied the Queen. 'If the evidence of your fervent love is to be credited. But so that I may be more sure, I would like to have your solemn oath to that effect, though I would mitigate it with this qualification – that if you come ever across a woman more beautiful, wiser and more accomplished than I, you may freely pledge her your faith and marry her.'

Her confidence in her own matchless gifts made her regard such an undertaking, deftly obtained by a kind of ambush, as a solemn oath never to remarry.

The King, his eyes swimming in tears, promised all that the Queen wished, and she died in his arms.

Never did any husband make such an outcry. To hear him sobbing night and day, you might have wondered how long he could keep up his mourning. You might even have thought he wept for his dead love like a man in a hurry to get the business over with.

You would not have been mistaken. After a few months he set about choosing a new wife.

However, this was no easy matter: he was obliged to keep his royal oath, and so the new bride must be more lovely and more charming than she whom he had so recently laid to rest. Neither the Court, where beautiful women abounded, nor the City could furnish such another; nor could the country-side, nor the surrounding kingdoms, of which he made an extensive tour. He realised at last that only the Princess was more beautiful than her mother, having certain graces, which the dead woman had not possessed.

Afire with a sudden intense passion for his own daughter, he was mad enough to convince himself, that because she was the only person who met the conditions of his vow, he must therefore marry her. He even found a casuist, who was prepared to give it as his opinion that the case might be made to stand up in court.

But the young Princess, horrified to be told of such a love, grieved and wept continuously. Her mind seething with a thousand anxieties she went to find her godmother, an admirable Fay, unequalled in her art, who lived far from the Court in a secluded grotto elaborately decorated with coral and mother-of-pearl.

'I know why you have come here,' she said on seeing the Princess. 'I know the deep distress in your heart, but you need not worry any more. Nothing can harm you now, as long as you allow yourself to be guided by my advice. True, your father wants to marry you, and it would be a great sin to listen to his insane demand, but it may be possible to refuse his suit without openly defying him.

'Tell him that before you yield your heart to his love, he must satisfy a desire you have for a gown the colour of the weather. In spite of all his wealth and power, even though Heaven itself favoured his wishes, he would not be able to fulfil such a condition.'

The young Princess went straightaway to her father, and trembling in her shoes, said what her godmother had suggested.

Within the hour he had called in the most notable tailors, and had informed them, that if they did not make for him a gown the colour of the weather (and without keeping him waiting too long either), they could be assured that he would have them all hanged.

The second day had not yet dawned, when they delivered the desired gown. The purest blue of the sky, girdled with clouds of gold, was not a more perfect shade of azure.

The Princess, torn between delight and distress, did not know what to say, nor how to free herself from her commitment.

Fortunately, however, her godmother was at her side.

'Princess, ask for another,' said the Fay in an undertone. 'Something more brilliant and less commonplace. Ask for a gown the colour of the Moon. He will not be able to give you that.'

But the Princess had hardly made her request, before the King said to his embroiderer:

'See that the stars of the night are not more splendid, and let me have it within four days without fail.'

The lavish garment was completed on the day appointed, and was just as the King had described it. The Moon in her silver robes, walking the Heavens where night has spread its veils, is not as stately as that gown seemed – not even when, surrounded by her attentive Court, her brighter radiance makes the stars look pale.

Wondering at this marvellous dress, the Princess could almost make up her mind to consent, but inspired again by her godmother, she said to the lovesick King:

'I still could not be quite happy, unless I had a yet more brilliant gown – the colour of the Sun.'

The King, who by now loved her with a passion beyond comparison, immediately sent for a wealthy jeweller, and commanded him to make a gown of regal cloth of gold and diamonds, saying that if the work were not completely satisfactory, he would have him tortured to death.

The King was excused the necessity of putting himself to so much trouble, for the hard-pressed craftsman delivered his priceless piece of work before the end of the week. It was so beautiful, so brilliant, so glowing, that the Sun-god himself, Climene's fair-haired lover driving his chariot across the vault of Heaven, never blinded the eyes with a more dazzling blaze of light.

Utterly disconcerted by these gifts, the Princess did not know how to reply to her father and King, but her godmother at once took her by the hand.

'There is no need to be trapped in such a pretty pass,' she whispered in her ear. 'Is it any wonder you receive these gifts, as long as he has the Ass, which as you know, fills his purse unfailingly with gold. Ask him for the skin of this rare beast of his. Since it's the source of all his wealth, you won't get *that*, or I'm very much mistaken.'

This Fay was a very learned lady, and yet she was unaware of the fact that a violent infatuation will count gold and silver for nothing, if only it can be satisfied. The hide was promptly and graciously granted to the Princess, the moment she asked for it.

When the skin was brought to her, it frightened the life out of her, and she cried out bitterly against her unhappy fate.

But at that moment the Fay appeared, ready as ever to advise and support her godchild. She reasoned that as long as one does the right thing, one need never be afraid. She made the Princess see that she must stop thinking about the King (for the poor girl was now quite resigned to marrying him). Instead she must fly immediately, alone and in disguise, to some distant land, since this was the only way to avert an evil so imminent and certain.

'I have here a large chest,' she went on, 'in which we will put all your clothes, your mirror, your dressing-table and your jewels. I am going to give you my ring as well. When you wear the ring, the chest will follow in your track, but always hidden underground. When you want to open it, you must touch the ground with this wand, and it will at once appear before your eyes.

'The donkey's hide will make a wonderful mask: you'll be quite unrecognisable. It's so frightful that if you keep well hidden in it, no one will ever imagine it could conceal anything beautiful.'

Thus camouflaged the Princess set out from the wise Fay's home in the freshness of the early morning.

She was hardly on her way, when the King, who was happily preparing to celebrate his wedding, learned of her flight. He was shattered by this dismal reversal in his fortunes. There was not a house, road or avenue that was not searched immediately, but all the excitement was in vain; no one could discover what had become of her.

A sad, black disappointment spread throughout the land: no wedding, no banquet, no cake, no sugared almonds. The ladies of the Court were all out of spirits, and most of them went right off their food. But the priest's disgruntlement was greater than anyone else's, for he finished up breakfasting very late, and worst of all did not have any collection to make up for it.

Meanwhile the Princess continued on her way, her face disfigured with a covering of dirt. She stopped everyone she met and tried to find a place as a servant. But even the least fussy and most unfortunate, seeing her looking so sullen and filthy, refused to listen to her, let alone take such a dirty creature into their homes. She travelled a long way, therefore, further and still further, until at last she came to an estate where the manager needed a slavey, whose talents need not extend to more than washing dishcloths thoroughly and cleaning the pigsty.

She was relegated to a dark corner of the kitchen, where the menservants did nothing but push her around, insulting her and jeering at her. The bumptious good-for-nothings never left her alone, harassing her at every turn and making her the customary target of all their coarse witticisms.

Only on Sundays did she have some peace and quiet, for once she had completed her small duties in the morning, she was able to go to her room, wedge the door shut and clean herself up. Then she opened her chest, set up her dressing-table and tidily arranged all her little pots on it. Happy and satisfied, she paraded in front of the big mirror, sometimes in the Moon gown, sometimes in the one which blazed like sunshine, sometimes in the beautiful blue dress, which all the azure of the skies could not match. The only flaw in her pleasure was that the room was too small for a long train to spread out fully. She enjoyed the sight of herself young and fair complexioned, a hundred times more elegant than any other girl could possibly be. This mild indulgence sustained her courage and carried her through to the next Sunday.

I forgot to mention in passing that this large estate housed the menagerie of a great and powerful King, who kept there a vast number of strange and exotic birds of every imaginable species, which filled at least ten courtyards.

The King's son often visited this fascinating place, to rest as he returned from the hunt and to take an iced drink with the Lords of his Court. His manners were regal and he had a soldierly appearance, which impressed the most experienced troops. Donkeyskin saw him from afar, and looked on him with kindness, realising from this temerity, that under her dirt and rags she still had the heart of a Princess.

'What a princely air he has, yet so informal,' she said. 'How attractive he is, and how very happy the lady must be to whom his heart is engaged! If he had honoured me so, I should think myself finer in the shabbiest clothes, than in all the beautiful gowns I have.'

One day as the young Prince wandered aimlessly from yard to yard, he passed through the dark passage, where Donkeyskin had her humble lodging, and happened to look through a crack in her door. As it was a holiday, she had put on one of her superb dresses, the one of cloth of gold and diamonds, rivalling the purest sunshine, and a set of priceless jewels.

The Prince gazed to his heart's content. Watching her like that, he could hardly draw breath, being so overwhelmed with delight. Marvellous as her dress was, the beauty of her face, her lovely figure, her fair complexion, her delicate features, her youthful freshness touched him a hundred times more. But it was a certain aristocratic air, and still more a seemly modesty, bearing witness to the beauty of her spirit, which completely took possession of his heart.

Three times in the heat of the fire which swept his senses, he would have forced open the door, but he believed that he was looking at a goddess, and awe stayed his hand.

He withdrew in a state of abstraction to the Palace, where he sighed night and day. He did not want to go to the ball, even though it was Carnival time. He suddenly detested hunting and the theatre. He lost his appetite, everything sickened him to the heart, and the root of his sickness was a dreary, deadly listlessness.

He inquired who the amazing girl was, who lived in the aviary, at the end of a frightful alley where you could not see a thing in broad daylight. 'That's Donkeyskin,' he was told, 'but there's nothing amazing or beautiful about her: she's called Donkeyskin because of the old hide she wears round her neck – a real cure for love, she is; the ugliest creature you ever saw, bar a wolf.' But it was all said in vain; he did not believe a word. The features engraved on his memory by love, were not to be so easily effaced.

Meanwhile the Queen his mother, who had no other child, was in despair. In vain she urged him to tell her what troubled him: he groaned, he wept, he sighed, but he would say nothing except that he wanted Donkeyskin to make him a cake with her own hands. His mother did not know what he meant.

'Oh Heavens, Madame!' said the people she asked about this. 'That Donkeyskin is a dreadful little black mole, uglier and filthier than the dirtiest monkey.'

'It doesn't matter,' said the Queen. 'He must have what he wants; that's all we must think about.'

If he had wanted to eat gold, his mother would have given it to him, she loved him so much.

When Donkeyskin received her orders, she took flour, specially sifted to make her pastry the finer, also salt, butter and fresh eggs, then she shut herself up alone in her little room to make her galette.

First she washed her hands, arms and face, and put on a silver bodice, so as to do her work in a fitting manner. She laced herself up quickly and set to work at once.

It is said that because she was working a little too hastily, one of her valuable rings fell into the dough; but some people, whom I believe to know the real ins and outs of the story, claim that she dropped it in on purpose. Frankly, for my part, I dare say this is true. At all events, I am sure that when the Prince approached her door and watched her through the crack, she was aware of him. Women are so perceptive in these matters, their eyes are so sharp, that it is impossible to look at them for a moment, without them knowing that they are observed. Moreover I am certain, indeed I would swear to it, that she had not the least doubt that the ring would be well received by her young lover.

Such a tasty delicacy as that galette had never been kneaded, and the Prince found it so good, that he nearly swallowed the ring as well in his greedy hunger. When he saw the wonderful emerald, however, and the narrow circle of its gold band, showing the form of the finger which had worn it, his heart was touched with incredible joy. In an instant he put it under his pillow.

But still his illness worsened, and the wise and experienced doctors, seeing him grow thinner from day to day, judged from their great learning, that he must be sick for love. As marriage (whatever may be said against it) is the best remedy for this disease, it was concluded that he ought to wed. When this suggestion had been put to him several times, he said at last:

'I would be very happy to marry, provided I can have the person, whom this ring fits.'

The King and Queen were most surprised by this eccentric demand, but he was so ill, that they dared not refuse.

So began the quest for the girl, whom the ring, regardless of birth, was to elevate to the highest place. There was not a woman in the country, who did not prepare to present her finger, or who would have forgone her right to try.

The news having gone forth, that it was necessary to have an extremely thin digit to have any hope of marrying the Prince, every charlatan made himself welcome by saying he had the secret of making fingers small. One woman had the bizarre idea of grating her finger like a carrot, another cut a little piece off hers, another thought she could make hers smaller by pressing it, and yet another made her skin fall off, by using a certain water, which was supposed to make fingers less fat. In short, there was absolutely no device, to which the ladies did not resort, in the hope of making their fingers fit the ring nicely.

The search began with the young Princesses, the Marquises and the Duchesses; but their fingers, though delicate, were all too thick and would not go in. The Countesses and Baronesses and all the noble ladies similarly presented their hands in turn, and presented them in vain.

Next came the citizens' daughters, whose pretty little fingers (for some were very attractive) sometimes looked as if they must fit the ring. But it was always too small or too large, and rebuffed the whole world with equal disdain.

At last it was necessary to try the servants, the cooks, the villagers, the goosegirls, all the little tiddlers in the pool, whose raw, grubby paws hoped for a happy destiny as much as the dainty hands. Many a girl presented herself with thick, stubby fingers, which would have passed through the Princess's ring as easily as a ship's cable through the eye of a needle.

Eventually it seemed as if the business was over, for indeed only poor Donkeyskin remained in a corner of the kitchen, but who could believe that Heaven had destined her to reign? 'And why not?' said the Prince. 'Bring her here.' Everyone began to laugh, exclaiming: 'What's the sense of having that dirty little ape brought in?'

But when she stretched out from under her grimy skin a little hand, which looked like ivory tinted with crimson, and when the fateful ring encircled her slender finger in a perfect fit, the Court was more surprised than you could imagine.

They were ready to carry her off at once to the King, in a transport of unexpected delight, but she asked that before being presented to her Lord and Master, she should have time to change into another dress. To tell the truth, everyone was prepared to laugh at this other dress (whatever would Donkeyskin's Sunday best be like?), but when she arrived in the State Apartments and passed through the reception rooms in her stately clothes, the elaborate splendour of which had never been equalled, all the ladies of the Court, charming and elegant though they were, faded into insignificance. Her lovely fair hair was dressed with diamonds, the brilliance of which made it shine like the sun; her blue eyes were wide and gentle, full of proud majesty, and never looked at anyone without delighting and wounding; her figure was so slender and dainty, that her waist might have been spanned with two hands.

Amid the joyful acclaim of the whole company, the King was stunned to see his daughter-in-law possessed of so much charm. The Queen was infatuated with her, and the Prince, her dear love, his heart overwhelmed with joy, almost fainted under the burden of his delight.

Everyone immediately began to prepare for the wedding. The Monarch invited all the Kings from the countries around, who left their own states to attend the great event, brilliant in their varied regalias. Some came from the regions of the Dawn, mounted on great elephants, whilst others came from Moorish shores. Indeed, Princes arrived from every corner of the earth, and the Court overflowed with them.

But no Prince nor potentate appeared there in such splendour as the father of the bride, who had once been in love with her himself. Time had purged the fire with which his fevered heart had blazed. He had banished all criminal desires, and the small trace of that odious flame which remained, merely strengthened his paternal love. As soon as he saw her, he said:

'Heaven is good to me, in allowing me to see you again, my dear child!'

And weeping with joy, he ran to embrace her tenderly.

Everyone wanted to share his happiness, and the bridegroom was delighted to learn that he was to be the son-in-law of so powerful a King.

At that moment the godmother arrived too, and told the whole story, covering Donkeyskin with glory by her recital.

The moral of this tale is not hard to find, for it is as plain as a child's lesson. It is better to expose oneself to the harshest adversity, rather than fail in one's duty. Though Virtue may suffer misfortune, it is always rewarded in the end.

This story shows too that the strongest reasoning is but a feeble dam against the wilful demands of a mad infatuation, and that love cannot be bought with expensive gifts.

Perhaps it also demonstrates that any young girl can live quite healthily on coarse bread and clear water – so long as she has fine clothes, and that there is not a single female under heaven, who does not believe herself to be beautiful; who does not imagine, moreover, that if she had been a participant in that famous beauty contest between the three goddesses, Paris would certainly have awarded the golden apple to *her*.

The tale of Donkeyskin may well strain credulity, but I think it will survive, as long as there are children to listen to stories, and mothers and grandmothers to tell them.

Dear Madame,

Were the morals I drew from 'Donkeyskin' really so many and so overwhelming? It was all simply for my own justification, I promise you; to prove that I was not wasting your time and my own with fantastic nonsense. I am full of remorse, that Mademoiselle should think I was charging her with vanity. What could have been further from my mind?

Will I be forgiven, do you think, by the time you return to Paris? I hope so, for I should not wish any cloud to dim the pleasure of that reunion. And after so long, it is to be so soon! It is just as well, because I have only one more story to hand. Since the time is so short, it is just as well too, that it is a very short story. The subject is very long, however.

If you and Mademoiselle were ladies of less rational intelligence, I should take good care not to tell you the silly and inelegant little fable I am about to relate. It concerns a mile of black pudding. Imagine telling a story like that to one of these affected ladies, who are so delicate-minded and serious, that they only want to hear about affairs of the heart. A mile of black pudding, my dear! How shocking!

But since you yourself know better than anyone alive, how to tell a story delightfully, I think you know that it is form more than matter, which gives beauty to any narrative. So I dare to believe with complete assurance, that you will like my last fable, and its moral . . .

The Ridiculous Wishes

THERE was once a poor woodcutter, who, weary of
his toilsome life, had a great desire (or so he said) to
go and rest forever in Elysium, for he claimed in his
profound melancholy, that as long as he had lived,
cruel Heaven had never chosen to fulfil a single one
of his wishes.

One day in the woods, when he began to bewail
his fate in this manner, Jupiter appeared to him,
thunderbolt in hand.

It would be difficult to depict the good man's
terror.

'I don't want anything. Really!' he said, throwing himself on the ground. 'No wishes, no thunder,
Lord. Let's just stay as we are.'

'There's no need to be afraid,' said Jupiter. 'Your complaint has hurt my feelings, and so I've come to make you see how badly you've wronged me. Now listen: I promise, I who am sovereign master of the whole world, to grant in full the first three wishes you choose to make, whatever they may concern. All right? Now you've got what you wanted, you've got the opportunity to make yourself happy – but remember: your happiness depends entirely on your wishes, so think very carefully before you make them.'

At these words Jupiter re-ascended into the skies. The carefree woodcutter hugged his great bundle of wood and slung it on his back to return home. The load had never seemed less burdensome.

'In all this I must do nothing lightly,' he said trotting along happily. 'It's an important matter. I must consult the wife.'

As he came into his thatched cottage, he said:

'Now Fanchon, let's build up the fire, sweetheart: we're rich forever, and we only have to make a few wishes.'

And he told her the whole story at length.

His wife was a lively, quick-witted girl. As soon as she heard his tale, a thousand grandiose projects came into her head, but considering the importance of behaving prudently, she said to her husband:

'Blaise, my love, let's not spoil things by our impatience. Let's discuss thoroughly between ourselves what to do in such a situation. Let's sleep on it and leave making our first wish until tomorrow.'

'I entirely agree,' said the worthy Blaise. 'Let's have some wine.'

When she returned with the wine, he drank at his ease by a big fire, he savoured the pleasure of relaxing, with the prospect of even greater luxury to come. Leaning back in his chair he said:

'While we've got such a good blaze going, a mile of black-pudding would be just the job!'

He had hardly finished pronouncing the words, when to her astonishment his wife saw a great long black-pudding coming out of the corner of the chimney and wriggling towards her like a snake. She screamed, but then, realising that this bizarre happening was a result of the wish, which her foolish husband had made out of sheer stupidity, she turned on him. There was no term of abuse or insult, which in her rage and resentment she did not heap on the poor man.

'We could have had an Empire,' she said. 'Gold, pearls, rubies, diamonds, lovely clothes – and you have to ask for a black pudding!'

'All right, I was wrong,' he said. 'I made a bad choice. I made a terrible mistake. I'll do better next time.'

'Fine, fine,' she said. 'Go and tell it to the marines! You must be as dumb as an ox to make a wish like that!'

The enraged husband had more than half a mind to wish in a whisper to be a widower (and maybe, between ourselves, he could have done worse).

'Men are born to suffer,' he said. 'Plague take the pudding. I wish to God it was hanging on the end of your nose, you stupid woman!'

Heaven at once heard his prayer. As soon as the words were uttered, the mile of black-pudding attached itself to the nose of his infuriated wife.

This unexpected miracle greatly upset her. Fanchon was pretty, indeed she was a very charming girl, and to tell the unvarnished truth, that particular ornament in that particular position did not do a great deal for her looks. Hanging as it did over the lower part of her face, it also prevented her from speaking easily, a marvellous advantage for a husband. It seemed such a good idea, in fact, that in that happy moment it did occur to him to ask for nothing more.

'After such a dreadful disaster,' he said to himself, 'I could well use the one wish I've got left to make myself King right away.'

It is true that there is nothing to equal royal grandeur, but then he had to consider how the Queen would feel, and what misery it would plunge her into, to put her on a throne with a nose a mile long. She had to be allowed to have her say in the matter, and decide whether, if she had the choice, she would rather become a great Princess and keep the horrible nose, or remain a woodcutter's wife with a nose, such as she had possessed before this misfortune befell her.

She knew, of course what powerful influence a sceptre has, and that when one wears a crown, one always has a perfect nose. But the desire to be attractive does not readily give way to any other consideration, and so, having thoroughly considered the thing, she preferred to keep her little peasant bonnet, than to be a Queen and be ugly.

Thus the woodcutter did not change his station in life at all. He did not become a great potentate, and no gold pieces filled his purse, for he was only too happy to use the wish that remained to restore his wife to her former condition (for all the good that did him).

. . . It is clear, then, that wretched humans, blind, imprudent, restless and changeable, are ill equipped to make wishes of this sort. There are few enough of them, who are capable of making use of the gifts Heaven bestows on them in the ordinary way.